Ancient Fragments

by I. P. Cory

INTRODUCTORY DISSERTATION.

IN presenting this collection of ANCIENT FRAGMENTS to the world, some explanation of what is comprehended under that title may not be deemed unnecessary. We are accustomed to regard the Hebrew scriptures, and the Greek and Latin writings, as the only certain records of antiquity: yet there have been other languages, in which have been written the annals and the historyies of other nations. Where then are those of Assyria and Babylon, of Persia and Egypt and Phœnicia, of Tyre and Carthage? Of the literature of all these mighty empires, where are even the remains? It will, no doubt, tend to excite some reflections of a melancholy cast, to look on this small volume as an answer. That all such remains are contained in it, I should be unwilling to assert: yet, with some diligence and research, I have not been able to increase its size with other fragments, which I could consider sufficiently authenticated.

It was my wish to have included in this collection all the fragments of the earlier Gentile world, which have reached us through the medium of the Greek language. Of the early historians of Greece the names only of some have come down to us; whilst of others, such as Eupolemus and Histiæus, several very interesting fragments have escaped the general wreck. In the classic ages of their literature, the acquaintance of the Greek historians with antiquity was generally confined and obscure: nor was it till the publication of the Septuagint, that they turned their attention to their own antiquities, and to those of the surrounding nations: and for this reason we meet with more certain notices of ancient history in the later, than in the earlier times of Greece. To have drawn a line then; to have inserted the earlier writers in exclusion of the later, would have been to have omitted the more valuable. To have reprinted the fragments of many authors, such as Nicolaus Damascenus, a writer of Damascus, of the Augustan age, would have introduced, with some matter worthy of attention, much of little interest. To have selected from them all, the passages relating to ancient times and foreign states, would have been a task as useless as laborious, and would have swelled the collection to a series of volumes. I have therefore, for the most part, excluded the native Greek historians—and every writer of the Augustan age and downwards—I have also omitted all fragments which bear about them the stamp of forgery, or are the productions of Hellenistic Jews, or of authors who have had access to the sacred Scriptures, and following the words, throw no additional light upon the subjects; under one or other of which divisions may be classed the Antediluvian books of Enoch, the fragments of Artapanus, the Sibylline Oracles, the Correspondence of Solomon and Hiram king of Tyre, the tragedy of Ezekiel in which Moses figures as the hero, with several compositions of a similar description.

The contents, then, of this volume, are Fragments which have been translated from foreign languages into Greek; or have been quoted or transcribed by Greeks from foreign authors; or have been written in the Greek language by foreigners who have had access to the archives of their own countries. Yet to render the collection more useful, and as it were a manual to the Chronologist and Mythological Antiquarian, I have added by way of Supplement such fragments and extracts as appear to have descended from more ancient sources, though they are now to be found only in the works of Greek or Latin writers. Some of these are merely illustrations of the fragments, or contain detached chronological notices, or such other curious information as may well be deemed worthy of a place. Thus I have endeavoured to comprise, in the volume, all the genuine relics of antiquity which precede the era of Grecian history; and which lie so scattered among the folios, chiefly of the Fathers and the Philosophers of the lower empire, as to be inaccessible to the Antiquarian, unless in the neighbourhood of some large public library.

Miscellaneous as such a collection might be at first supposed, it will be found to resolve itself into two subjects; the early History, and the ancient Theological Systems of the world. In the following pages I have endeavoured to present a sketch of both; not with a view of entering into the details, but rather as a method of connecting the fragments with one another, to facilitate an examination of their contents, by directing the attention successively to those great landmarks which stand prominently forth amidst what might otherwise be deemed a wild, pathless and interminable; and to enable the reader, by following the same order of perusal, to elicit something like a regular continued narrative. In the Scriptures we have a brief but authenticated account of the earliest ages: but among the heathen writers, with the exception of some few very valuable historical fragments, we have little more than a collection of allegories and legendary tales. Upon examination, however, most of these legends, notwithstanding their obscurity, will be found to contain references to those grand primeval events whose memory was retained among every people upon earth: and for the commemoration of which were ordained so many of the ceremonies and mysteries of the ancients.

From such traditions, handed down for ages before they were committed to writing, we might expect but little aid. Indeed in all the researches of the antiquarian, conjecture must very generally supply the place of science. Yet, by pursuing a proper method of investigation, we may approximate to truth, and frequently illustrate circumstances obscurely hinted at in Scripture, and even occasionally fill up the gaps of history, by supplying events which have been omitted by the sacred writers as unconnected with the immediate objects under their consideration.

Persons, Events, and Dates in History, and Systems in Theology, are the objects to be examined and ascertained. And where the subject under investigation can be so divided, that the truth must lie among some few plausible hypothesis, which can be a priori, and at once laid down: by collecting an the evidence that can be had, and examining separately, and excluding soccessively each of these hypothesis which shall be found inconsistent with that evidence, we may conduct the circle of conjecture, in some cases, till but one hypothesis is left; which one must be the truth, and is thus negatively rendered matter of demonstration. In other cases want of evidence may leave room for several different opinions, none of which can really be refuted, though one may often be more plausible than another.

Mr. Faber, in his admirable work on the Pagan Idolatry; has collected and separately examined all the different systems of the Heathen Mythology; and has shown, 'that there is such a singular, minute, and regular accordance among them, not only in what is *obvious* and *natural*, but also in what is *arbitrary* and *circumstantial*, both in *fanciful speculations* and in *artificial observances*,' as to render untenable every other hypothesis than this—'that they must all have originated from some common source.'

Having thus shown their common origin, he enumerates three hypothesis as the only three on which, he conceives, the common origination of the various systems of Paganism can be accounted for:

.   Either all nations agreed peaceably to borrow from one, subsequent to their several settlements.

.   Or all nations, subsequent to their several settlements, were compelled by arms to adopt the superstition of one.

Or all nations were once assembled together in a single place and in a single community; where they adopted a corrupt form of religion, which they afterwards respectively carried with them into the lands that they colonized.

After examining at length and shewing the utter impossibility of maintaining either the first or second of these hypothesis, he concludes that the third only can be the truth.[1]

In the same manner we may ascertain the region from which mankind originally dispersed. Both in ancient and modern times the Greeks have been accused of a kind of plagiarism, which was the prevailing custom of every nation upon earth. Egypt and India, and Prœnicia, no less than Greece, have appropriated to themselves, and assigned within their own territorial limits, the localities of the grand events of primeval history, with the birth and achievements of the Gods and Heroes, the Deluge, the origin of the arts and the civilization of mankind. And their claims have found more able supporters, only because they have not been so obviously liable to refutation. Yet by rejecting each country, whose claims rest upon no better foundation than its own local histories, and retaining those only, whose pretensions are substantiated by the concurrent testimony of the rest;

---

[1] To these, perhaps, may be added a fourth, viz. that the superstition became general, partly by peaceful communication, and partly by force of arms: though the fulness of the evidence is such as to render this equally untenable with the others.

it may be shown, independently of Scripture, that the primitive settlements of mankind were in such places, and attended with such circumstances, as the Scripture instructs us was the case.

Of the transactions previous to the Deluge there are but few and faint memorials among the heathens. One of the most authentic may be found in the remains of the Prœnician History of Sanchoniatho, who is considered to be the most ancient writer of the heathen world. In what age he wrote is uncertain: but his history was composed in the Prœnician language, and its materials collected from the archives of the Prœnician cities. It was translated into Greek by Philo Byblius, and for the preservation of these fragments we are indebted to the care of Eusebius.

The Cosmogony I shall have occasion to refer to hereafter: as one of the most ancient, it is extremely valuable, and as it speaks more plainly than the rest, it affords a key to their interpretation.

The Generations contain many very curious passages. In the first is an allusion to the fall: in the second Genus may be Cain: after which we lose the traces of similarity: at the fifth there is an interruption. But taking up the thread of inquiry, at the end, in Taautus or Thoyth, we may recognize Athothis, the second king of Egypt, the Hermes Trismegistus, who againt appears as the adviser of Cronus. His predecessor Misor then corresponds with Mizraïm, the first king of Egypt, the Menes and Mines of the dynasties. In the preceding generation is Amynus,

Amon, or Ham, the same with the Cronus, of what by the historian is supposed to be a different but contemporary line. An ascent higher we find, Agrus, the husbandman, who was worshipped in Phœnicia as the greatest of the gods: he corresponds with Noah, the Ouranus of the other line, whose original name was Epigeus or Autochthon.

Sanchoniatho seems to have been a very diligent inquirer, and intimates at the conclusion that the generations contain the real history of those early times, stripped of the fictions and allegories with which it had been obscured by the son of Thabion, the first hierophant of Prœnicia. That such is the case, we are assured by Philo Byblius, in the remarks on Sanchoniatho with which he prefaces his translation of the work. The passage also informs us that the history thus disguised was handed down to Isiris, the brother of Chna the first Prœnician, apparently alluding to Mizraïm the brother of Canaan.

It is very remarkable that he has placed these characters in the true order of succession, though in all the traditions of the heathens they are generally confounded with one another. It is also remarkable that Sanchoniatho is almost the only heathen writer upon antiquities who makes no direct mention of the deluge, though several obscure allusions to it may be found in the course of the fragment. Were we assured of his silence upon the point in the parts of his work that have been lost, the omission might still be accounted for from his avowed determination to suppress what he considered merely allegorical, for he would find the traditions of the deluge so intimately blended with those relating to the creation, that in endeavouring to disengage the truth from the fable he might easily be induced to suppose that they related to the same event.

For explanation of his fragment upon the mystical sacrifice of the Prœnicians, I must refer to the very curious dissertations by Bryant and Mr. Faber. Sanchoniatho wrote also a history of the serpent, a single fragment of which is preserved by Eusebius.

In the fragments of Berossus again we have perhaps some few traces of the antediluvian world. Like Sanchoniatho, Berossus seems to have composed his work with a serious regard for truth. He was a Babylonian by birth, and flourished in the reign of Alexander the Great, and resided for some years at Athens. As a priest of Belus, he possesscd every advantage which the records of the temple and the learning and traditions of the Chaldæans could afford. He appears to have sketched his history of the earlier times from the representations upon the walls of the temple. From written and traditionary knowledge he must have learned several points too well authenticated. to be called in question; and correcting the one by the other, and at the same time blending them as usual with Mythology, he has produced the strange history before us.

The first fragment preserved by Alexander Polyhistor is extremely valuable, and contains a store of very curious information. The first book of the history apparently opens naturally enough with a description of Babylonia. Then referring to the paintings, the author finds the first series a kind of preface to the rest. All men of every nation appear assembled in Chaldæa: among them is introduced a person age who is represented as their instructor in the arts and sciences, and informing them of the events which had previously taken place. Unconscious that Noah is represented under the character of Oannes, Berossus describes him, from the hieroglyphical delineation, as a being literally compounded of a fish and a man, and as passing the natural, instead of the diluvian night in the ocean, with other circumstances indicative of his character and life.

The instructions of the Patriarch are detailed in the next series of paintings. In the first of which, I conceive, the Chaos is pourtrayed by the confusion of the limbs of every kind of animal: the second represents the creation of the universe: the third the formation of mankind: others again that of animals, and of the heavenly bodies.

The second book appears to have compre- hended the history of the ante-diluvian world: and of this the two succeeding fragments seem to have been extracts. The historian, as usual, has appropriated the history of the world to Chaldæa. He finds nine persons, probably represented as kings, preceding Noah, who is again introduced under the name Xisuthrus, and he supposes that the representation was that of the first dynasty of the Chaldæan kings. From the universal consent of history and tradition he was well assured that Alorus or Orion, the Nimrod of the Scriptures, was the founder of Babylon and the first king: consequently he places him at the top, and Xisuthrus follows as the tenth. The destruction of the records by Nabonasar left him to fill up the intermediate names as he could: and who are inserted, is not easy so to determine.[2]

Berossus has given also a full and accurate description of the deluge, which is wonderfully consonant with the Mosaic account. We have also a similar account, or it may be an epitome of the same from the Assyrian history of Abydenus, who was a disciple of Aristotle, and a copyist from Berossus. I have given also a small extract from the Fragments of Nicholaus Damascenus, relative to the deluge and the ark, whosc wreck is said by him as well as Berossus, Chrysostom, and other writers, to have remained upon Ararat even at the very time in which they wrote.

Mankind appear to have dwelt some time in Armenia, and the Patriarch allotted to his descendants the different regions of the earth, with commands to separate into distinct communities. His injunctions, however, were disobeyed, and great numbers, perhaps all the human race, started from Armenia in a body, and, according to the Scriptures,

---

[2] In the Syriac Chronicle of Bar-Hebræus, the names in the catalogue are given to certain recluses of the line of Seth, called the Sons of God, who lived upon Mount Hermon, and afterwards apostatized and became the fathers of the Giants.

journied westward, but according to Berossus, travelled by a circuitous route to the plains of Shinar. By combining the two narratives, we may conclude that they followed the winding course of the Euphrates, till they halted upon those celebrated plains, where the enterprising spirit of Nimrod tempted him to aspire to the dominion of the world, and to found the Tower and City of Babel as the metropolis of his future universal empire.

Upon the Tower of Babel and the events connected with it, will be found some very interesting fragments from Abydenus, from Hestiæus, a very ancient Greek writer, from the Babylonian Sibyl, and from Eupolemus. I have added also a curious extract from the Sibylline oracles. In these fragments are detailed the erection of the Tower, the dispersion of its contrivers, and the confusion of the languages; with the additional circumstances of the violent destruction of the building,[3] and the Titanian war, which forms so remarkable an event in all traditions of the heathens.

Previously to the erection of the Tower, men appear very generally to have apostatized from the patriarchal worship. About this time a further

---

[3] Upon the rebuilding of Babylon, the Tower was completed most probably on the original plan. It is described by Herodotus as a pyramid of eight steps, about seven hundred feet high. Its ruins, which are still known upon the spot as the Birs Nembrod, or the tower of Nimrod, are described by Sir R. K. Porter, as a prodigious pile of unburnt bricks cemented with mud and reeds in horizontal layers, still rising to the enormous height of about two hundred and fifty feet.

deviation from the truth took place; and upon the first and more simple corruption was engrafted an elaborate system of idolatry. Some account of these deviations will be found in the extracts from Epiphanius, Cedrenus, and the Paschal chronicle. What is mentioned under the name of Barbarism, was probably the primeval patriarchal worship. It was succeeded by a corrupted form of superstition which is known among the ancients under the name of Scuthism, or Scythism, which was most prevalent from the flood to the building of the Tower. The new corruption, at that time introduced by Nimrod, was denominated Ionism,[4] or Hellenism: and both are still flourishing in the East under the well-known appellations of Brahmenism and Buddhism; whose priests appear to have continued in an uninterrupted succession from the Brahmanes and Germanes, the philosophical sects of India mentioned by Megasthenes and Clitarchus.

By the introduction of a more degenerate superstition, Nimrod appears to have aimed at the establishment of an universal monarchy in himself and his descendants, of which Babylon was to have been the metropolis, and the Tower, the central temple of their idolatries. All who attended him seem to have entered into the project, so far as he might have thought proper to divulge it, and to have assisted in the erection of the tower and city. But

---

[4] Most probably derived from Ione: for the worship of the great Goddess,or universal Mother, was then introduced, as well as Idolatry. It signifies also a Dove, which was the standard of the Assyrian Empire.

subsequent events shew that the proposed form of government and system of theology, though asquiesced in by the majority, did not command universal approbation. And the whole project was marred by the miraculous interposition of the Almighty.

What concurring circumstances might have operated to the dispersion, we have no clue to in the narrative of Moses. He mentions the miraculous confusion of the languages, and that the Lord scattered the people abroad from thence upon the face of all the earth; and they left off to build the city. But if we may credit the heathen accounts above referred to, with which the Hindoo, and indeed almost every remnant of traditionary lore concur; a schism, most probably both of a political and religious nature, was the result; a bitter war was carried on, or at least a bloody field was fought; from which the Scuths, defeated and excommunicated by their brethren, betook themselves, in haughty independence, to the mountains of Cashgar and the north:[5] whilst some violent and supernatural catastrophe, by the overthrow of the Tower, completed the dispersion.

The Scythic nations became very generally Nomade, but sometimes settled in various parts. Of what family they were has been a subject of long and intricate dispute. The ancient chronologists have, almost without exception, supposed them of the race of Japhet, the eldest son of Noah: that they were the sons of Cush has also been insisted on with great

---

[5] See Faber, Lib. VI. c. 4.

16

learning and ingenuity.[6] But if all the nations, or even the upper classes of those nations, which bear the name, be the sons of Cush, one-third of the present human race must be the descendants of that patriarch. Indeed, before the introduction of Ionism, Epiphanius and others appear to have included all mankind under the name of Scuths. The first apostacy might have been introduced by Cush, and its followers have borne his name; which the succeeding heresy of Nimrod could not obliterate.

The Scythian nations of Touran and the North were generally addicted to the Scythic superstition; and whenever they rolled back the tide of war upon their ancient rivals; the idols temples and cities were the objects upon which they satiated their revenge. They

---

[6] The term Scuth, which, with the prefix, is supposed to be the same as Cuth or Cush, the root of the names Chusas Chasas Cassians Cusæans or Chrusæans, Chusdim Chasdim or Chaldæans, Cotti or Goths and many others, appears too general for a patronymic. All the northern nations were Scuthic, the Scuths of Touran. The Scuths of Iran occupied the entire Asiatic Ethiopia, containing the Iranian territories of the Assyrian Empire, extending from the Euphrates to the Indus, and from the Caspian to the Ocean. African Ethiopia or Nubia with the adjoining territories was also Cuthic. There were Indo-Scythæ, Celto-Scythæ, and even Ionic-Scythæ. The Belgæ in Gaul, the Pelasgi in Greece, the Sacas or Saxons, the Pelestim Philistim and Prœnicians, the Sarmans Sarmatians and Germans were Scuths. In short, the term is to be found in every corner of the earth, and may be traced in America and in Lapland, as well as in China and Japan.

were esteemed excommunicated, and of the Giant race, Nephelim, Rephaim and Anakim. The Scuths of Iran were also of the Giant race, with Nimrod as their chief. Of the Titanian war there appears to be a double aspect. When the Scuths of Touran are the Giants, the war between them and the Ionim is the subject of the legend; and they are the Giants cast out into Cimmerian darkness, and buried under mountains. The other view presents both parties conjointly before the schism, as the Nephelim, Apostates or Giants, engaged in carrying on the war against Heaven itself. And in these accounts we find more frequent allusions to the Tower and its supernatural overthrow.

The catastrophe at Babel completed the dispersion. On the division of the earth and planting of the nations, there are some very curious notices extant. But whether Nimrod and his immediate adherents survived, and retained possession of Babylon, or transferred their seat of government to Nineveh and founded the great Iranian empire, or whether that empire and city were founded by Assur and the sons of Shem, is still a subject of dispute. We find Nimrod, however, under the well-known title of Alorus, at the head of the two Chaldæan dynasties, mentioned above: but these appear rather to refer to the antediluvian patriarchs than to the proper kings of Chaldæa.

The first dynasty of Chaldæan Kings is placed by almost all chronologists as the first Iranian dynasty, that of Nimrod under the name of Evechius, and his immediate descendants. Evexius is also placed by Polyhistor as the first Chaldæan king. The dynasty of the Arabian kings of Chaldæan is placed by Eusebius, Syncellus and others, as well as by Berossus, next in the order of succession. They have likewise been supposed to be a Scythic nation, which broke in upon the empire from the Scythian settlements of Cashgar, and obtained possession either of the entire empire, or only of the city of Babylon, during the period of its desolation, with the plains of Shinar and the country round the head of the Persian gulf, from whence they were expelled, and discharged themselves upon Palestine as the Palli or Philistines, and upon Egypt as the Hycsos or Shepherd Kings.

Next in succession, according to Eusebius and Syncellus, or perhaps contemporary with the preceding, came the long line of the great dynasty of the Assyrian Kings, who held the empire of the world for ten or twelve centuries, till their dominion was wrested from them by the Medes in the time of Thonus Concolerus, the Sardanapalus of the Greek historians. The different catalogues of the great Assyrian succession that are extant, will be found among the Dynasties. The overthrow of the Assyrian empire was followed by several years of universal anarchy, bloodshed and revolution. And it is ascertained, that it was during this scene of confusion that Jonah was sent upon his mission to stop its progress at Nineveh.

Arbaces, the leader of the Median insurrection, though he succeeded in throwing off the Assyrian yoke, appears to have failed in his attempt to establish his own sovereignty: nor was the Median kingdom fully consolidated till the reign of Deïoces. The catalogues of the Median kings will be found among the Dynasties. Under Phraortes and Cyaxares the Medes extended their dominion over great part of Asia, but under Astyages, who was defeated and captured by Cyrus, the kingdom merged in the Persian empire.

The Babylonians acquired a temporary independence at the fall of the Assyrian empire, but after two or three short reigns they were subdued by Senecherib. Syria also became an independent kingdom, and prospered for a time, till again reduced under the Assyrian yoke. Persia at the same time arose, and alone maintained its independence against the growing power of the Medes and the new Assyrian dynasty, till the successes of Cyrus raised it above them all, and vested the empire of the world in the Persian race.

The Assyrian empire revived under Nabonasar, supposed to be the same with the Salmanasar of the Scriptures. Of this dynasty three several catalogues will be found, the Ecclesiastical and Astronomical canons preserved by Syncellus, and the celebrated canon of Ptolemæus, besides some other notices of the successors of Nabonasar, among the supplemental Chaldæan fragments. The first princes of the line appear to have fixed their residence at Nineveh, and among them we may recognize the Tiglath Pileser, Senecherib, and Esar Haddon of the Scriptures. Their race appears to have terminated in Saracus, another Sardanapalus. Nabopollasar, a successful rebel, began the last line of the Assyrian and Chaldæan monarchs. He transferred the seat of empire to Babylon, and in his reign, his celebrated son, Nebuchadnezzar, extended his conquests over the bordering kingdoms of the north and west, by the reduction of Syria, Phœnicia, Judæa, Egypt, and Arabia; an accurate account of which is transmitted by Berossus. On the death of his father, Nebuchadnezzar succeeded to the throne. Concerning him we have several very interesting fragments from Berossus, and one from Megasthenes. In these are detailed the splendor of his works at Babylon, its celebrated walls, and brazen gates; its temples, palaces, and hanging gardens. The prophesy of Nebuchadnezzar, probably alludes to the public notification of Daniel's interpretation of his vision. His successors, till the overthrow of the empire by Cyrus, are given by Berossus and Megasthenes, and will be found also among the dynasties. Among his four immediate successors we must find Belshazzar, and Darius the Mede. The latter has been generally supposed to be Nabonnedus, though some have endeavoured to identify him with Cyaxares. The conquest of the Median, Chaldæan, and Assyrian dominions by Cyrus, grandson of Astyages, and the nephew of Nebuchadnezzar, brings down the history to the authentic records of Grecian literature. The Persian line, the successors of Cyrus, will be found in several different places, both among the Chaldæan and Egyptian fragments.

The intense interest which Egyptian history has excited, from the discovery of the interpretation of the Hieroglyphics, has induced me to spare no labour or expence in rendering this part of the work as perfect as circumstances would allow.

The Laterculus or Canon of the Kings of Thebes, was compiled from the archives of that city, by Eratosthenes, the librarian of Ptolemæus Philadelphus. It is followed by the Old Egyptian Chronicle, with a Latin version of the same, from the Excerpta Barbara, and another from the Armenian Chronicle of Eusebius: they contain a summary of the dynasties of Egypt. To these succeed the Egyptian dynasties of Manetho, whose introductory letter to king Ptolemæus, given in a subsequent page, explains the nature of his work, and the materials from whence it was compiled. I have placed the six different versions of the Dynasties of Manetho that are extant confronting each other. The Canon of the kings of Egypt from Josephus, I have compiled from the historical fragments of Manetho: and I have thrown it into the form of a Canon to facilitate comparison. I have next given a very important Canon, the first part of which, from Mestraim to the end of the seventeenth dynasty, is preserved by Syncellus only: from the beginning of the eighteenth it is continued also in the fragments of Eusebius: and from hence to the conclusion, four different versions of it will be found. To these are added the Canons of all the kings of Egypt, mentioned by Diodorus Siculus and Herodotus. They were originally compiled by Scaliger, but I have corrected them and given them with several very important additions in the original words of the authors, instead of in the words of Scaliger himself. They are followed by the Canon of Theophilus Antiochenus. And after several very important chronological extracts upon the antiquities of Egypt, I have completed the Dynasties, with a Canon of the early Egyptian, Chaldæan, and Assyrian Kings, from the Syriac Chronicle of Bar-hebræus: which I have placed beside each other as they are synchonized by that author, and given them in the English letters corresponding to the Syriac, instead of adopting the Latinized names of the translators.

I have, therefore, comprised in this part of the work, no less than nineteen catalogues of the Egyptian kings, with all the various readings that occur in the different versions of the same. They have been compiled with the greatest care, and I have purposely abstained from all reference to the Hieroglyphics, that I might not be misled by any preconceived opinion.

At a time, when indefatigable research is every day bringing to light new and interesting circumstances, it would be absurd to attempt to give anything but the roughest outline of Egyptian history. I shall merely observe, then, that after the dispersion from Babel, the children of Mizraim went off to Egypt, of which they appear to have continued some time in undisturbed possession. Menes Misor or Mestraim, the Mizraim of the Scriptures, and planter of the nation, is naturally placed as the first sovereign of the united realm, at the head of all the catalogues. And perhaps the dominion of Athothis was equally extensive; for his name occurs in the Laterculus of Eratosthenes, and as the Thoth or Taautus of Sanchoniatho. After him the country seems to have been divided into several independent monarchies, some of whose princes may perhaps be found among the fourteen first dynasties. That the country was so divided, and that the first dynasties were not considered successive by the ancients, we have the authority of Artapanus and Eusebius.

The first historical fragment of Manetho, from Josephus, gives an account of the invasion and expulsion of a race of foreigners, who were styled Hycsos or Shepherd kings; whose princes are identified with the seventeenth dynasty of all the Canons except that given hy Syncellus as the canon of Africanus, in which they are placed as the fifteenth. Of what family they were, whence they came, and to what country they retired, have heen the subjects of almost as many hypotheses as writers; I shall not venture a remark upon a prohlem, of which there is every reason shortly to expect a satisfactory solution. Josephus and the Fathers confound them with the Israelites, who appear rather to he referred to by the second fragment as the lepers, who were so cruelly ill-treated by the Egyptians, and afterwards laid waste the country, assisted by a second invasion of the Shepherds. To these fragments I have subjoined six other very curious notices of the exodus of the Israelites and the final expulsion of the Shepherds; which events appear to have been connected with one another, as well as with the emigration of the Danaan colonies to Greece, not only in time, but hy circumstances of a political nature, and to have occurred during the sovereignty of the eighteenth dynasty. Tacitus has also noticed the exodus, but in terms evidently copied from some of those which I have given: we have but few and scanty notices of the kings of Egypt, even in Diodorus and Herodotus. Its conquest by Nebucchadnezzar is related by Berossus, and after two or three temporary gleams of independence, it sunk at length into a province of the Persian empire, and from that day to the present, according to the denunciation of the prophet, Egypt has been the basest of kingdoms, and under the yoke of strangers.

The Tyrian Annals are fragments which were quoted by Josephus from the lost histories of Dius and Menander. They agree perfectly with the scriptural accounts, and furnish some particulars in addition. The correspondence of Solomon and Hiram, the foundation of Carthage, and the invasion, conquests, and repulse of Salmanasar; the siege of Tyre by Nebuchadnessar, and its subsequent government under judges, are historical additions of great interest and importance.

The Periplus of Hanno is an account of the earliest voyage of discovery extant. It was taken from an original and apparently official document which was suspended in the temple of Saturn, at Carthage. Falconer has edited it as a separate work, and gives two dissertations on it; the first, explanatory of its contents; and the second, a refutation of Dodwell's reflections on its authenticity. I have followed

Falconer both in his text and translation. With respect to its age, Falconer agrees with Bougainville in referring it to the sixth century before the Christian era.

The Periplus is prefaced by a few lines, reciting a decree of the Carthaginians, relative to the voyage and its objects: and is then continued by the commander, or one of his companions, as a narrative, which commences from the time the fleet had cleared the Straits of Gibraltar. Bougainville has given a chart of the voyage, which may be found, togetherwith the corresponding maps of Ptolemæus and D'Anville, in Falconer's treatise. It may be sufficient, however, to remark that Thymiaterium, the first of the colonies planted by Hanno, occupies a position very nearly, perhaps precisely the same with that of the present commercial city of Mogadore. The promontory of Soloeis corresponds with Cape Bojador, nearly opposite to the Canaries. Caricontichos, Gytte, Acra, Melitta and Arambys are placed between Cape Bojador and the Rio d'Ouro which is supposed to be the Lixus. Cerne is laid down as the island of Arguin under the southem Cape Blanco: the river Chretes perhaps is the St. John, and the next large river mentioned is the Senegal. Cape Palmas and Cape Three Points, are supposed to correspond respectively with the Western and Southern Horns, and some island in the bight of Benin,. with that of Gorillæ. Vossius, however, supposes the Western Horn to be Cape Verd, and the Southem, Cape Palmas, in which case the Sierra Leone will answer to the Ochema Theon the Chariot of the Gods.

The description of the Troglodytæ, as men of a different form or appearance, may imply a change from the Moresco to the Negro race. Some passages, quoted by Falconer from Bruce's travels, explain the extraordinary fires and nightly merriment which alarmed the voyagers, as customs common among many of the negro tribes, and which had repeatedly fallen within the scope of his own observations. The Gorillæ are supposed to be large monkeys or wild men as the name ἄνθρωποι ἄγριοι may in fact import.

The Periplus is followed bya strange account of the African settlements, from the books of Hiempsal king of Numidia, preserved by Sallust.

Of the Indian fragments of Megasthenes, the most remarkable has already been referred to. In the two great divisions of the Philosophical sects, into the Brahmanes and Germanes, we may doubtless recognize the predecessors of the present Brachmans and Buddhists of Hindostan. They are likewise mentioned by Clitarchus as the Brahmanes and Pramnæ. The castes of India are also described at length, and have continued with some variations to the present day. The antiquity of such a division is very great, and perhaps originated at the dispersion, as it prevailed chiefly among the Ionic nations, while the Scythic tribes prided themselves upon their independence, and the nobility of the whole race. Megasthenes is reputed to have been a Persian, and an officer in the army of Alexander in his expedition to India, and was employed upon several negociations of consequence.

I have next given two short notices of some celebrated islands in the Atlantic and Indian oceans. The first, upon the Atlantic island, is quoted by Proclus, from the Ethiopic history of Marcellus, in illustration of the passages of Plato in the Timæus relative to the same. Some have looked upon the relation as worthy of credit, and confirmed by the broken nature of all the islands, which lie scattered between the old and the new world, regarding them as relics of a former tract which has been absorbed. The second fragment from Euemerus may relate to the islands in the Indian Archipelago; though it is highly probable that both may refer only to the White island of the West, so celebrated in the Mythological legends of almost all nations, and in none more than in the antiquities of the British islands.

As I profess not to enter into the details, but merely to provide as it were the raw materials, I shall dwell but little upon Chronology. By far the most authentic record that has come down to us is the Canon of Ptolemæus. It commences from the Chaldæan era of Nabonasar, and is continued to the conclusion of the reign of Antoninus Pius. In calculating its chronology, however, it must be observed, that although it starts from this Chaldæan era, its years are the Sothoic years of Egypt, consisting only of three hundred and sixty-five days, without any intercalation. Among the Chronological fragments at the end of the work will be found the passage of Censorinus, so important in determining the celebrated epochs of ancient history; and likewise an extract from Theon Alexandrinus, from the manuscripts of the King of France, partly cited by Larcher in his translation of Herodotus.[7] For the complete extract, I beg leave to return my thanks to Mons. Champollion Figeac, and Mons. Hase librarian to the king. Several useful chronological passages will be found scattered over the work: some also are collected at the end of the Dynasties. I have added also two short notices of the Sarus and Nerus of the Chaldæans.

It is remarkable, that the three great eras of ancient history commence within thirty years of one another, and are commonly fixed.

The first Olympiad, B. C. 777.

The foundation of Rome, B. C. 753.

And the era of Nabonasar, B. C. 747.

The commencement of the reign of Dioclesian is determined by the observed and calculated eclipses to be in the year A. D. 284. The beginning of the great Sothoic period of 1641, Sothoic or vague years, equivalent to 1640 Julian years, is fixed about the year B. C. 1321, or 1325. During this great embolismic period, the first day of the Egyptian year, called Thoth, from the omission of the intercalation of the quarter of a day in each year, recedes through every day of the year, till it arrives at the point whence it originally started, and again coincides with the Heliacal rising of the Dogstar.

---

[7] Vol. ii. p. 556.

Having thus brought down the ancient history of the world as contained in the fragments to the times of Grecian record, I shall endeavour, in like manner, to trace a faint outline of its Theology.

From Babel, the centre of their abominations, the heathens carried off the same objects of adoration, the same superstitious observances, and the same legendary tales, which, however varied and confused, may without difficulty be identified throughout the world. Among the pastoral tribes, the Scythic doctrines almost universally prevailed; yet in subsequent times they also fell into idolatry: while the Ionic nations carried their additions and corruptions to such a length, that the original and more simple doctrines became obliterated among the vulgar; and were retained only by the philosophers and priests, and sometimes were even re-imported from abroad. The more elaborate corruptions of Ionism appear to have prevailed originally in the Iranian territories only, and to have passed to India and to Egypt, to have spread themselves with civilization over Greece, and subsequently over the whole Roman world. By foreign conquest and other circumstances, the two systems were often amalgamated into one. The more elaborate and corrupted form of Ionism and idolatry would catch the attention of the casual observer as the religion of the land; while the deeper doctrines, which retained much of their primitive simplicity, were wrapped in mystery, and communicated only to the initiated.

Most nations, in process of time, became more attached to particular parts, and retained but fragments of the general system. But it is still in existence, and preserved almost entire, both in its Scythic and Ionic form, as the Buddhism and Brahmenism of Hindostan. By comparing all the varied legends of the west and east in conjunction, we may obtain the following outline of the theology of the ancients.

It recognizes, as the primary elements of all things, two independent principles, of the nature of male and female. And these, in mystic union as the soul and body, constitute the great Hermaphroditic deity, the One, the Universe itself, consisting still of the two separate elements of its composition, modified, though combined in one individual, of which all things were regarded but as parts. From the two, or more frequently from the male, proceeded three sons or Hypostases; which, when examined severally, are each one and the same with the principle from which they sprung: but when viewed conjointly, they constitute a triad, emanating from a fourth yet older divinity, who, by a mysterious act of self-triplication, becomes three, while he yet remains but one, each member of the triad being ultimately resolvable into the monad.[8] With this is connected the doctrine of a succession of similar worlds. At the conclusion of each revolving period, the world is dissolved, alternately by flood and fire; and all its varied forms and parts are absorbed into the two primeval principles, which then remain in the loveliness of

---

[8] See Faber at length upon this subject, Pag. Id. Vol. II.

their existence. After a certain interval their re-union commences, and with it the reconstruction of another world. As before, the first production of this world is the triad, and the same heroes and persons re-appear; and the same events are again transacted, till the time arrives for another dissolution. Such was the system in its original form; it was a foundation of materialism, upon which was raised a superstructure of idolatry.

The most remarkable feature in the heathen theology is the multiplicity of its gods. The easy temper of polytheism, as it has been called, hesitated not to adopt the divinities of the surrounding nations; while the deification, not only of heroes and kings, but of the virtues and vices, with the genii of the woods and waters, mountains and cities, contributed to introduce new and strange inmates into the Pantheon. But if we eject these modern intruders, if we restore to their original seats the imported deities, such as Pan to Arcadia, Dermes to Egypt, Osiris to Memphis, Hercules to Tyre, and Dionysus to India; and if we investigate the origin of each, we shall find every nation, notwithstanding the variety of names, acknowledging the same deities and the same system of theology: and, however humble any of the deities may appear in the Pantheons of Greece and Rome, each, who has any claim to antiquity, will be found ultimately, if not immediately, resolvable into the original God or Goddess, into one or other of the two primeval principles.

In conducting such an investigation, a very singular circumstance presents itself in the manifold character of these deities. Their human or *terrestrial* appearance, as mere mortals deified is the most obvious; as the sun, moon, elements, and powers of nature, they assume a *celestial* or *physical* aspect. And if we turn to the writings of the philosophers, we shall find them sustaining a character more abstract and *metaphysical*. Yet under all these different forms, the same general system is preserved.

In his *terrestrial* character, the chief Hero God, under whatever name, is claimed by every nation as its progenitor and founder. And not only is he celebrated as the king of that country in particular, but of the whole world. He is exposed to some alarming danger from the sea, or an evil principle or monster by which the sea is represented. He is nevertheless rescued by some friendly female aid, sometimes concealed in a cavern or in the moon, or preserved in a death-like sleep, borne upon a snake, or floating on an island or a lotus, though more frequently in a boat or ark. At length he awakens from his slumber, subdues his enemy, and lands upon a mountain. He then reorganizes the world, and becomes himself the father primarily of three sons, and through them, of the human race; not unfrequently with some allusions to the dove and rainbow. In fact, in his human character he was the great father of mankind; but he may not only be identified with Noah but with Adam likewise. The one was looked upon as the re-appearance of the other, and both an incarnation of the Deity.

In his immediate *celestial* character the God is universally held to be the Sun; but the character of the great Goddess is of a more complex description. As the companion of the man, she is the ark; which was regarded not onlyas his consort, but his daughter, as the work of his own hands; and his mother, fromwhose womb he again emerged, as an infant, to a second life; and his preserver during the catastrophe of the deluge. As the companion of the Sun she is either the earth or moon: not that the distinctions between the human and celestial characters are accurately maintained; for they are so strangely blended together, that the adventures applicable to one are frequently, and sometimes purposely, misapplied to the other. Thus, whilst the Man is said to have entered into, been concealed in, and have again issued from the ark, the moon, and the earth, indifferently, the Sun is fabled to have been plunged into the ocean, to have sailed upon a lotus, to have taken refuge in a floating island, and to have dwelt upon a sacred mountain left dry by the retiring flood.[9]

It has been often remarked, that the Theogonies and Cosmogonies of the heathens were the same. In addition to those naturally constituting a part of the work, I have given the most remarkable of the Hermetic, Orphic, and Pythagorean accounts; which will be found, with the celebrated collection from Damascius, under a separate head. By comparing these with the Cosmogonies of Sanchoniatho, Berossus, and the rest, we may, without much difficulty, arrive at the following conclusion: that the

[9] See Faber, Pag. Id.

Ether and Chaos, or, in the language of the Philosophers, Mind and Matter, were the two primeval, eternal, and independent principles of the universe; the one regarded as a vivifying and intellectual principle, the other as a watery Chaos, boundless, and without form: both which continued for a time without motion, and in darkness. By a mystic union of the two was forrned the great Hermaphroditic deity, the One, the universal World; of which the Chaotic matter presently became the body, and the Etherial Intellectual principle the soul. As soon as the union had commenced, from the Ether sprung forth the triad, Phanes or Eros, a triple divinity, the most prominent character of which was Light. He was the same with the Soul of the World, and the Intelligible triad so largely insisted upon by the Platonists. The gross chaotic elements of Earth and Water were formed into the terraqueous globe, while the disposing Ether, in the character of Phanes, under some three of the conditions of Light, Air, Heat, Fire, Ether, Flame, or Spirit, composed a physical trinity concentred in the Sun, the soul and ruler of the world. Or, according to the more refined speculations, it consisted of a trinity of mental powers, in which the Understanding, Reason or Intellect, the Soul, Passions, Feelings or Affections, Power, Counsel or Will, are variously combined. Viewed, therefore, either under a physical or metaphysical aspect, it is still a triad subordinate to, and emanating from the more ancient Intellectual

Ether, and into which each person of the triad is again resolvable.[10]

With respect to the Physical triad, by comparing the heathen accounts with similar passages in the Scriptures, though not decisive, yet so preponderating does the evidence appear to me upon this point, that if the school of Hutchinson had not failed to establish their very elegant hypothesis, as to the fact that the Fire, Light, and Spirit or Air, were only three different conditions of one and the same etherial fluid, appearing as Fire at the orb of the Sun, as Light proceeding from it, and as Spirit returning to it, I should not have hesitated to subscribe to the opinion that such was the original trinity of the Gentiles; a triad, nevertheless, subordinate to a monad, which existed in the form of Ether previously to its assuming such conditions.

The Metaphysical speculations of the ancients upon this subject can only be derived by analogical reasoning from contemplation of the microcosm of man. To point out the close analogy preserved in this particular between the Metaphysical and Physical system before explained I would observe, that Man is a being compounded of an Intellectual, and of a Material substance, both of which were canceived by the ancients to have *pre-existed*, before they became united in the compound individual animal, the Man.

---

[10] See the Inquiry at the end.

When thus united, they appear to have conceived a triad of intellectual powers, the Intellect, the Affections Feelings or Emotions, and the Will or Power of action. But for further illustration of these matters, and for such proof as can be produced, I must refer to the disquisition at the end.

Upon this subject, therefore, I cannot agree with Mr. Faber in supposing that the trinitarian speculations of the Heathens originated in the coincidence of Adam and Noah being each the father of three sons; for of the three distinct analogical systems the Metaphysical, of the Mind with its Faculties, and Matter, — the Physical, of the Ether with its conditions, and the Chaos, — and the Human, of the Patriarch with his three sons, and the universal mother the Ark or Earth, — the last analogy is not only the most imperfect, but according to all historical accounts, Demonolatry was introduced subsequently to the worship of nature and the elements.

From the widely dispersed traditions upon the subject, it is manifest that the circumstances of the creation and the deluge were well known to all mankind previously to the dispersion. And the writings of Moses give to the chosen people, not so much a new revelation as a correct, authenticated and inspired account of circumstances, which had then become partially obscured by time and abused by superstition. The formless watery Chaos and the Etherial substance of the heavens, enfolding and passing over its surface as a mighty wind, are the first principles both of the sacred and profane cosmogonies; but they are reclaimed by Moses as the materials, created by the immediate agency of an Almighty power. The subsequent process of formation so completely corresponds in both systems, that if they were not borrowed the one from the other, (a position which cannot be maintained,) they must each have been ultimately derived from the common source of revelation. Similar considerations upon the traditions of a Trinity, so universal among the nations, and an examination of what that Trinity was composed, forces upon me the conviction, that the trinitarian doctrine, as it is now believed, was one of the original and fundamental tenets of the Patriarchal religion; that the analogy between the Microcosm, as pointed out, and the then current accounts of the creation, became the stumbling block, which set mankind to refine upon the truth; that hence they fell into the errors of attributing eternity to matter, of placing a Monad above the Trinity, with the Pantheistic opinion that the Deity was no other than the universe itself. The doctrine of the succession ofworlds, the Metempsychosis, and Demonolatry would follow naturally enough by an extension of their system from the particular circumstances of the creation to those attendant upon the deluge. By the pride of false philosophy they forsook the truth of revelation, and sunk into materialism, into the worship of the elements, of man and beasts, and into idolatry with all its attendant abominations. 'When they knew God, they glorified him not as God; neither were thankful; but became vain in their imaginations, and their foolish heart was darkened. Professing themselves to be wise, they became fools; and changed the glory of the incorruptible God into an image made like to corruptible man, and to birds, and four-footed beasts, and creeping things. Wherefore, God gave them up to uncleanness through the lusts of their own hearts.'[11]

To reclaim a world so fallen, the great manifestations of the Almighty from time to time have taken place. not only at the most civilized as well as celebrated periods of history, but upon the spots then best calculated for the general dissemination of truth among the heathens. The geographical situation of Palestine, chosen it may be for the seat of universal empire, is the most remarkable upon earth for the facility of communication which it affords with every quarter of the globe. At the time of the Advent, it formed as it were the boundary of the rival empires of Rome and Parthia, subject to Rome. but holding an intimate connexion with its colonial offspring within the Parthian dominions. And its situation was at that time not more excellently adapted for the universal diffusion of the Gospel, both in the East and West, than it was for the general instruction of mankind, in times of old, when it formed so considerable a part of the high road of communication between the empires of Egypt and Assyria. About the time of the eighteenth dynasty, the most brilliant I epoch of Egyptian history, the Exodus of the Israelites was effected: and the fame of the miraculous exploits of Moses and Joshua was wafted with the Danaan colonies to Greece, with the fugitive Canaanites to the

---

[11] Romans, i. 21.

West, and carried by the Israelites themselves into the East. During the revolutionary violence consequent upon the downfall of the ancient Assyrian empire, the same merciful Providence kept up a communication with the kingdoms which sprung out of its ruins, by the mission of Jonah to Nineveh, by the connexion of the princes of Samaria with Syria, and by the dispersion of the ten tribes over the territories of the Medes and Assyrians by Salmanasar: and upon the full re-establishment of the empire at Babylon, a knowledge of the truth was diffused far and wide by the captivity of the Jews themselves.

The conversion of Nebuchadnezzar, and the decrees of himself and his successors, both of the Assyrian and Persian line, in favour of the truth, must have been attended with at least some temporary effect upon the religious and philosophical sentiments of the East. And such an effect may be clearly traced in the very general reformation of the systems and superstitions which about this period took place.

Among the Persians, themselves a Scythic people, this reformation appears to have re-animated their zeal and enmity against the temples and idolatry of their Ionian rivals. It may also have led them to convert the two independent principles of Mind and Matter into spiritual agents in opposition to one another, and to have revived the unmingled worship of the Sun and Fire, at first but as an emblem and image of the Supreme, though it soon again degenerated into the Sabaism of old. The reformation may be traced through Assyria, India, China and

Egypt, and in those amendments and refinements which were shortly afterwards imported by Pythagoras into Greece.

A summary of the Pythagorean doctrines will be found in the commencement of the celebrated treatise of Timæus Locrus. It may be observed, that the Pythagorean speculations have a tacit reference to the ancient classification of Causes, as the Efficient, the Formal or Ideal, the Material and the Final. In conformity to this division we find introduced between the two ancient independent principles of Mind and Matter, the world of Forms or abstract Ideas, to which is attributed an eternal subsistence, if not an existence independent of the Mind; whilst the τἀγαϑὸν Good in the abstract, the summum bonum, the great final cause, became the subject of perpetual discussion and inquiry among all succeeding philosophers.

The Forms and Matter were now substituted for the ancient Duad; superior to which was placed the Efficient Cause as the Monad, Deity, or Demiurgus. This Duad was, nevertheless, regarded as two eternal and independent principles, and by their combination the Deity formed the Sensible world, a living animal, composed of soul and body. Subordinate to the duad is the Pythagorean Triad, occupying the same relative situation with respect to the duad as in the more ancient systems. By this introduction of the Ideal world, and the elevation of the deity above the duad, the system lost something of the gross materialism which had hitherto obtained, but it lost, at the same time, all knowledge of the ancient triad, which was now replaced by such triads as were more conformable to the Pythagorean mode, and of which the persons were often subordinate to, or comprehended within each other, as genera and species.

The doctrines of Plato differ only in refinement from the preceding. If we admit the Parmenides and the Timæus to embrace his complete system, God and Matter, two originally independent principles, are held to be, as it were, the extremities of that chain of being which composes the universe. Subordinate to the God, we have the Intelligible world of Ideas or the Forms, commencing, as the latter Platonists insist, with the Intelligible triad: but whether Plato regarded this world of Ideas in the abstract as subsisting only *within* the mind of the Deity, or whether he attributed to it a distinct existence[12] *without* the Mind, comprehending different orders of divine super-essential beings, may well be questioned. When the Deity or Demiurgus thought proper to compose the world, he looked to this ideal world as the exemplar, in whose likeness he constructed his new work. He impressed the disordered material Chaos with the Forms, and rendered the world a living animal, after the pattern of its ideal prototype, consisting of a soul

---

[12] Existence, according to the ancients, implies essence; whereas the Ideal world was deemed super-essential: but I am compelled to use the words to make myself understood; for the English language has not been sufficiently accommodated to these metaphysical subtleties of the Greeks to supply the requisite terms.

endued with Intellect, and of a body of which all beings comprehended in it, Gods Men Animals or material species, are but the concrete individuals, of which the abstract ideas unalterably subsist in the intelligible world. Though still supposed to continue in existence, the Deity, as in the more ancient systems, retires as effectually from the stage as did the ancient Ether when superseded by the Phanes. And all the mundane operations are carried on as before, by the Soul of the world.

While the Stoics and other schools retained the ancient doctrines, and looked not further than the world itself, it is true that the Pythagoreans and Plato held a God superior to the world; but it is extremely doubtful whether they entertained a sublimer conception of their great immediate efficient cause, the Soul of the world, or indeed of Soul in general, than the gross materialism of a subtile ether. They discouraged, likewise, the tenet of the succession of worlds; though it was subsequently revived by the later Platonists, by whom the Deity was supposed, at the predestined time, to swallow up the world, first the sensible, then the Ideal, and lastly Phanes the Intelligible triad, and to remain in the solitude of his unity.

Much as has been said upon the Platonic trinity I must confess that I can find fewer traces of that doctrine in the writings of Plato than of his less refined predecessors, the mythologists. I have given such extracts as appear to me to relate to the subject, together with a fragment of Amelius which expressly mentions the three kings of Plato as identical with the Orphic trinity. Dr. Morgan, in his essay upon the subject, satisfactorily refutes the notion, that Plato regarded the Logos as the second person of the trinity:[13] and upon this refutation he denies that Plato

---

[13] The celebrated passage in the Epinomis of Plato Ξυναποτεγῶν χόσμον ὃν ἔταξε λόγος ὁ πάντων θειότατος ὁρατόν, usually rendered, "Perfecting the visible world, which the word, the most divine of all things, made," refers to a very different subject. The inquiry in this part of the dialogue relates to the knowledge of number, without which it is asserted a man cannot have λόγος *reason*; and if destitute of reason, he cannot attain wisdom. The God, which imparted to man the knowledge of numbers, is the Heaven, for there are eight powers contained in it akin to each other, that of the Sun, of the Moon, &c. to whom, he says, must be assigned equal honour — "For let us not assign to one the honour of the year, to another the honour of the month, and to others none of that portion of time, in which each performs its course in conjunction with the others, accomplishing that visible order which reason, the most divine of all things (or of the Universe.) has established.

The no less celebrated passage from the Philebus, Ὅτι νοῦς ἔστι γενούστης τοῦ πάντων αἰτίου, by which it is supposed that the consubstantiality of the Logos with the first cause is asserted, relates to the *human mind,* and is the conclusion of an argument which proves, that as ordinary fire is derived from the elemental, and the human body from the elemental body of the world, *so is the human mind akin to, or of the same nature with the Divine mind, or Soul of the universe, the cause of all things*. These and other less celebrated passages of Plato, when examined in conjunction with this context, afford us, as Dr. Morgan justly observes, no more foundation for supposing that Plato held the doctrine of the Trinity than the following very curious passage, which he produces from Seneca, gives us ground to suppose that it was held by the Stoics: "Id actum est, mihi crede ab illo, quisquis formator universi filit, sive ille *Deus* est *potens omnium*, sive

held the doctrine at all, more particularly, as from the time of Plato to that of Ammonius Saccas in the third century, no disciple of his school seems to have been aware that such a doctrine was contained in his writings. Perhaps, however, we may trace some obscure allusions to it in the beginning of the second hypothesis of the Parmenides and in the passages which I have given; though in the latter the doctrines appear rather to refer to the Monad and Duad than to the genuine trinity of the ancients. So far from any such doctrine being maintained by the Pythagoreans or in the Academy, we find only such vague allusions as might be expected among philosophers, who reverenced an ancient tradition, and were willing, after they had lost the substance, to find something to which they might attach the shadow.

The error which Dr. Morgan has refuted, took its rise with the fathers of the Church in the second century. They were led into the mistake by the word

---

incorporalis ratio ingentium operum artifex, sive *divinus spiritus* per omnia maxima minima, æquali intentione diffusus, sive fatum et immutabilis causarum inter se cohærentium series."14 To the observations from Dr. Morgan's work, I may venture to add that the word Logos, as used by St. John and Plato, has two very distinct significations. By the latter, Reason in general is implied, whereas St. John uses it as a translation of the Hebrew DBR, the Word signifying also a thing or person revealed, and if at all in the sense of reason, which may be implied from the commentaries of the fathers, not for reason in general, but for the particular faculty so called.

Logos, used by Plato and St. John, and made the Platonic Trinity to consist of God, the Logos, and the Soul of the world, and this in spite of all the professed followers of Plato, who, however they might vary among themselves, uniformly insisted upon placing the Monad and Duad, or at least a Monad, above their Triad.

In the first century of the Christian era, Philo, an Alexandrian Jew, had attempted to expound the Scripture on Platonic principles; and after the promulgation of the Gospel many of the fathers warmly adopted the same mode of exposition. The different sects of the Gnostics went far beyond the Grecian sage, and sought in the East the doctrines, to which they looked upon the writings of Plato merely as essays, introductory to the sublimer flights of the Oriental mysticism: and they treated his followers with that contempt, against which the vanity of a philosopher is seldom proof; and as long as these schools existed, a bitter enmity prevailed between them. The Gnostics gave at once a real *existence* to the Ideal world, and continuing the chain of being from the Supreme, through numerous orders of Eons, personified abstract ideas, of which the second and third persons of the Trinity were the first and second Eons, and from thence to the lowest material species, founded that daring heresy which so long disturbed the tranquillity of Christendom: and with this spurious Platonism of the fathers the Arian[14] heresy is likewise intimately connected.

But the internal heresies of the Church were not the only ill effects which the misguided zeal of the fathers, in forcing upon Plato the doctrine of the Trinity, brought about. Though it is possible, that by pointing out some crude similarity of doctrine, they might have obtajned some converts by rendering Christianity less unpalatable to the philosophical world of that day, yet the weapon was skilfully turned against them, and with unerring effect, when the Pagans took upon them to assert that nothing new had been revealed in Christianity; since, by the confessions of its very advocates, the system was previously contained in the writings of Plato.

In the third century, Ammonius Saccas, universally acknowledged to have been a man of consummate ability, taught that every sect, Christian, Heretic or Pagan, had received the truth, and retained it in their varied legends. He undertook, therefore, to unfold it from them all, and to reconcile every creed. And from his exertions sprung the celebrated Eclectic school of the later Platonists. Plotinus, Amelius, Olympius, Porphyrius, Jamblichus, Syrianus, and Proclus, were

---

[14] It is curious to observe the Arian and Orthodox illustrations of Eusebius and Epiphanius. The former illustrates the Trinity by the Heaven, the Sun, and the Spirit; or the Heaven, the Sun, and the Moon, the two latter as the leaders of innumerable host of spirits and stars, evidently derived from the prevailing notions of the Fathers relative to the Platonic trinity; whilst Epiphanius declares, that this great mystery is properly understood as Fire, Light, and Spirit or Air reveal it to us.

among the celebrated professors who succeeded Ammonius in the Platonic chair, and revived and kept alive the spirit of Paganism, with a bitter enmity to the Gospel, for near three hundred years. The Platonic schools were at length closed by the edict of Justinian; and seven wise men, the last lights of Platonism, Diogenes, Hermias, Eulalius, Priscianus, Damascius, Isidorus and Simplicius retired indignantly from the persecutions of Justinian, to realize the shadowy dreams of the republic of Plato, under the Persian despotism of Chosroes.[15]

From the writings of these philosophers is collected the bulk of the Oracles of Zoroaster. A few of them were first published by Ludovicus Tiletanus at Paris, with the commentaries of Pletho, to which were subsequently added those of Psellus. Chief part of them, however, were collected by Franciscus Patricius, and published with the Hermetic books at the end of his Nova Philosophia. To the labours of Mr. Taylor we are indebted for the addition of about fifty more, and for the references to the works from whence all were extracted. I have arranged them according to the subjects, which are said to be occultly discussed in the Parmenides of Plato, viz.: Cause or God, the Ideal Intelligible or Intellectual world, Particular Souls, and the Material world. And I have placed under a separate head the Magical and Philosophical precepts and directions. There can be no question but that many of these Oracles are spurious; all those, for instance, which relate to the

---

[15] For the particulars of this philosophical transaction see Gibbon, c. xl.

Intelligible and Intellectual orders, which were confessedly obtained in answers given by dæmons, raised for that purpose by the Theurgists;[16] who, as well as all the later Platonists, made pretensions to magic, not only in its refinements, which they were pleased to designate Theurgy, but also in that debased form which we should call common witchcraft. Nevertheless, several of the Oracles seem to be derived from more authentic sources, and, like the spurious Hermetic books which have come down to us, probably contain much of the pure Sabiasm of Persia, and the doctrines of the Oriental philosophy.

I have thus endeavoured to give I fear a very imperfect outline of ancient history and theology. But, as it is intended rather to assist the reader through such an heterogeneous heap of materials, by bringing forward the most prominent parts and connecting them with one another, I trust its errors will be excused, as they may be corrected by the readers better judgrnent from the materials themselves before him. In closing the subject, I beg to offer my sincerest thanks to Isaac Cullimore, Esq., to whose deep and extensive chronological researches, I am indebted for references to several very important passages in the following work, which had escaped my notice.

It is needless to take notice of the numerous forgeries, which have been issued as the productions

---

[16] The Theurgists were the two Julians, the father called Chaldæus, the son, Theurgus. They flourished in the reign of Marcus Antoninus, and were the first who delivered the oracles upon the Intelligible and Intellectual orders.

of the authors of these fragments. There is a complete set, which was composed in Latin by Annius, a monk of Viterbo. But it is a singular circumstance, and one which might be urged with great force against the genuineness of almost the whole collection, that not only the original works have perished, but those also, through whose means these relics have been handed down. With the exception of these fragments, not only have Sanchoniatho, Berossus, and the rest passed into oblivion; but the preservers of their names have followed in the same track, and to a more unusual fate. The fragments of Philo, Abydenus, Polyhistor, Dius, and others, are generally not those of their own works, but extracts from their predecessors.

It is necessary also to advert to the numerous errors which will be found in every sheet. The fragments have been exposed to more than the common risks and accidents, to which all ancient writings have been subject. They have been either copied from the rude annals of antiquity, or sketched from historical paintings or hieroglyphic records, they have been sometimes translated from the sacred into the common language of the place, and again translated into Greek; then passed in citation from hand to hand, and lie widely scattered over the works principally of the fathers, and the writers of the Lower empire. It is matter of surprise then, not that they abound in error and uncertainty, but that so much of them has been preserved.

Several of these fragments are to be found in two or three different authors, each of whom contains a different version of the same, differing, not so much in the outline, and in the general flow of words, as in those technicalities and variations of termination, which were necessary to adapt them to the author's style; and it has been a source of some little perplexity to determine which of these various readings to prefer.

To Eusebius, Syncellus and Josephus, we are largely indebted for these relics of antiquity. For Josephus I have followed Hudson's edition. The Cologne edition of the Præparatio Evangelica of Eusebius is often considered the best: but upon close inspection and comparison I have been induced to prefer the text of Stephanus. With the exception of a mutilated translation into Latin by Hieronymus, Eusebius' Chronicle was lost. Under that title, however, Scaliger compiled a very portly folio, which, with some other Chronicles, contains a collection of all the fragments of the Greek text of Eusebius, that could be found. The recovery of the Armenian translation of this Chronicle is a great acquisition. It is regarded upon the Continent as perfectly authentic; but I am not aware that it has been examined or reviewed in England. To compress as much as possible all unnecessary observations upon the subject of materials, editions and abbreviations, I have given at the end a list of the authors cited, which will answer at once the several purposes of an index to the abbreviations, and to the editions I have used or referred to, as well as to the manuscripts and other sources from which some of those editions have been formed, or which have been consulted in the compilation of the work. I have likewise given it the form of a Chronological index, by adding the times in which the authors referred to flourished, that the reader may judge what degree of credit may be reposed in each.

The matter contained in these fragments is the only merit to which they can pretend. I have chosen what appeared to me the most genuine text, independent of all theory and system, and have given all the various readings of any consequence I have met with. I have retained Mr. Falconer's translation of Hanno's Periplus; and with this exception, and some few of the most obscure of the oracles of Zoroaster, which are due to Mr. Taylor, I must be answerable for the rest. For the many errors in which they must abound, I beg leave to apologize and claim indulgence. The broken and confused state of many of the fragments, preclude the possibility of giving any translation, except upon conjecture. Many, such as the Orphic fragment from Malala, and that from Amelius, have exercised the talent and ingenuity of some of the ablest commentators, none of whom perhaps will be found to agree. In such cases, I have patiently compared their opinions, and endeavoured to investigate the circumstances under which the fragments were written and have been preserved, and what connexion they have with the passages among which they are introduced, and to give, what to the best of my judgment is, the truth.

At the conclusion of this work I have added a disquisition, which was originally designed merely to explain and illustrate what I conceive to have been the ancient Trinity of the Gentiles: but in the progress of inquiry I found it impossible to do justice to the opinion without speaking largely upon ancient and modern science. To compress it, therefore, as much as possible, and to give it something of a connected arrangement, I have thrown it altogether into the form of an inquiry into the Method, Objects and Result of ancient and modern Philosophy. And, as in this work I have endeavoured to bring forward several historical and theological documents, which had, in a manner, retired from public view, I trust that such an inquiry will not be deemed altogether misplaced, and that I shall be excused in an attempt to draw from the same store-house of antiquity some speculations, which have been too generally slighted or overlooked by the Metaphysician and the Philosopher, but which I believe may tend to the advancement of science, even amid the brilliant discoveries of modern times.

With respect to the fragments themselves, the classical reader will find, I fear, but poor amusement in perusing a half barbarous dialect, replete with errors and inconsistencies: to the student of divinity, however, they may not be altogether unacceptable or devoid of interest: and to the inquirer after ancient history and mythology, it must be useful to have collected into one small volume, the scattered relics for which he must otherwise search so widely.

THE
THEOLOGY OF THE PHŒNICIANS:
FROM
SANCHONIATHO.

THE COSMOLOGY

HE supposes that the beginning of all things was a dark and condensed windy air, or a breeze of thick air and a Chaos turbid and black as Erebus: and that these were unbounded, and for a long series of ages destitute of form. But when this wind became enamoured of its own first principles (the Chaos), and an intimate union took place, that connexion was called Pothos:[17] and it was the beginning of the creation of all things. And it (the Chaos)[18] knew not its own production; but from its embrace with the wind was generated Môt; which some call Ilus (Mud), but others the putrefaction of a watery mixture. And from this sprung all the seed of the creation, and the generation of the universe.

And there were certain animals without sensation, from which intelligent animals were produced, and these were called Zophasemin, that is, the overseers of the heavens; and they were formed in the shape of

---

[17] This union, among the Heathens, and particularly among the Phœnicians, was symbolized by an Egg enfolded by a Serpent, which *disjunctively* represented the Chaos and the Ether, but, when *united*, the hermaphroditic first principle of the Universe Cupid or Pothos.

[18] "Wind knew not, &c." Vig. Col. Orel. Cumb. &c.

an egg: and from Môt shone forth the sun, and the moon, the less and the greater stars.

And when the air began to send forth light, by its fiery influence on the sea and earth, winds were produced, and clouds, and very great defluxions and torrents of the heavenly waters. And when they were thus separated, and carried out of their proper places by the heat of the sun, and all met again in the air, and were dashed against each other, thunder and lightnings were the result: and at the sound of the thunder, the before-mentioned intelligent animals were aroused, and startled by the noise, and moved upon the earth and in the sea, male and female. (After this our author proceeds to say:) These things were found written in the Cosmogony of Taautus, and in his commentaries, and were drawn from his observations and the natural signs which by his penetration he perceived and discovered, and with which he has enlightened us.

(Afterwards, declaring the names of the winds Notus, Boreas, and the rest, he makes this epilogue:) — But these first men consecrated the productions of the earth, and judged them gods, and worshipped those things, upon which they themselves lived, and all their posterity, and all before them; to these they made libations and sacrifices. (Then he proceeds: — Such were the devices of their worship in accordance with the imbecility and narrowness of their souls.) — *Euseb. Præp. Evan.* lib. I. c. 10.

THE GENERATIONS.

Of the wind Colpias, and his wife Baau, which is interpreted Night, were begotten two mortal men, Æon and Protogonus so called: and Æon discovered food from trees.

The immediate descendants of these were called Genus and Genea, and they dwelt in Phœnicia: and when there were great droughts they stretched forth their hands to heaven towards the Sun; for him they supposed to be God, the only lord of heaven, calling him Beelsamin, which in the Phœnician dialect signifies Lord of Heaven, but among the Greeks is equivalent to Zeus.

Afterwards by Genus the son of Æon and Protogonus were begotten mortal children, whose names were Phôs, Pûr, and Phlox. These found out the method of producing fire by rubbing pieces of wood against each other, and taught men the use thereof.

These begat sons of vast bulk and height, whose names were conferred upon the mountains which they occupied: thus from them Cassius, and Libanus, and Antilibanus, and Brathu received their names.

Memrumus and Hypsuranius were the issue of these men by connexion with their mothers; the women of those times, without shame, having intercourse with any men whom they might chance to meet. Hypsuranius inhabited Tyre: and he invented huts constructed of reeds and rushes, and the papyrus. And he fell into enmity with his brother Usous, who was the inventor of clothing for the body which he made of the skins of the wild beasts which he could catch. And when there were violent storms of rain and wind, the trees about Tyre being rubbed against each other, took fire, and all the forest in the neighbourhood was consumed. And Usous having taken a tree, and broken off its boughs, was the first who dared to venture on the sea. And he consecrated two pillars to Fire and Wind, and worshipped them, and poured out upon them the blood of the wild beasts he took in hunting: and when these men were dead, those that remained consecrated to them rods, and worshipped the pillars, and held anniversary feasts in honour of them.

And in times long subsequent to these; were born of the race of Hypsuranius, Agreus and Halieus, the inventors of the arts of hunting and fishing, from whom huntsmen and fishermen derive their names.

Of these were begotten two brothers who discovered iron, and the forging thereof. One of these called Chrysor, who is the same with Hephæstus, exercised himself in words, and charms and divinations; and he invented the hook, and the bait, and the fishing-line, and boats of a light construction; he was the first of all men that sailed. Wherefore he was worshipped after his death as a God, under the name of Diamichius. And it is said that his brothers invented the art of building walls with bricks.

Afterwards, of this race were born two youths, one of whom was called Technites, and the other was called Geïnus Autochthôn. These discovered the method of mingling stubble with the loam of bricks, and of baking them in the sun; they were also the inventors of tiling.

By these were begotten others, of whom one was named Agrus, the other Agrouerus or Agrotes, of whom in Phœnicia there was a statue held in the highest veneration, and a temple drawn by yokes of oxen: and at Byblus he is called, by way of eminence, the greatest of the Gods. These added to the houses, courts and porticos and crypts: husbandmen, and such as hunt with dogs, derive their origin from these: they are called also Aletæ, and Titans.

From these were descended Amynus and Magus, who taught men to construct villages and tend flocks.

By these men were begotten Misor and Sydyc, that is, Well-freed and Just: and they found out the use of salt.

From Misor descended Taautus, who invented the writing of the first letters: him the Egyptians called Thoor, the Alexandrians Thoyth, and the Greeks Hermes. But from Sydyc descended the Dioscuri, or Cabiri, or Corybantes, or Samothraces: these (he says) first built a ship complete.

From these descended others; who were the discoverers of medicinal herbs, and of the cure of poisons and of charms.

Contemporary with these was one Elioun, called Hypsistus, (the most high); and his wife named Beruth, and they dwelt about Byblus.

By these was begotten Epigeus or Autochthon, whom they afterwards called Ouranus (Heaven); so that from him that element, which is over us, by reason of its excellent beauty is named heaven: and he had a sister of the same parents, and she was called Ge (Earth), and by reason of her beauty the earth was called by the same name.

Hypsistus, the father of these, having been killed in a conflict with wild beasts, was consecrated, and his children offered libations and sacrifices unto him.

But Ouranus, succeeding to the kingdom of his father, contracted a marriage with his sister Ge, and had by her four sons, Ilus who is called Cronus, and Betylus, and Dagon, which signifies Siton (Bread-corn,) and Atlas.

But by other wives Ouranus had much issue; at which Ge, being vexed and jealous of Ouranus, reproached him so that they parted from each other: nevertheless Ouranus returned to her, again by force whenever he thought proper, and having laid with her, again departed: he attempted also to kill the children whom he had by her; but Ge often defended herself with the assistance of auxiliary powers.

But when Cronus arrived at man's estate, acting by the advice and with the assistance of Hermes Trismegistus, who was his secretary, he opposed himself to his father Ouranus, that he might avenge the indignities which had been offered to his mother.

And to Cronus were born children, Persephone and Athena; the former of whom died a virgin; but, by the advice of Athena and Hermes, Cronus made a scimitar and a spear of iron. Then Hermes addressed the allies of Cronus with magic words, and wrought in them a keen desire to make war against Ouranus in behalf of Ge. And Cronus having thus overcome Ouranus in battle, drove him from his kingdom, and succeeded him in the imperial power. In the battle was taken a well-beloved concubine of Ouranus who was pregnant; and Cronus bestowed her in marriage upon Dagon, and, whilst she was with him, she was delivered of the child which she had conceived by Ouranus, and called his name Demarous.

After these events Cronus surrounded his habitation with a wall, and founded Byblus, the first city of Phœnicia. Afterwards Cronus having coneived a suspicion of his own brother Atlas, by the advice of Hermes, threw him into a deep cavern in the earth, and buried him.

At this time the descendants of the Dioscuri, having built some light and other more complete ships, put to sea; and being cast away over against Mount Cassius, there consecrated a temple.

But the auxiliaries of Ilus, who is Cronus, were called Eloeim, as it were, the allies of Cronus; being so called after Cronus. And Cronus, having a son called Sadidus, dispatched him with his own sword, because he held him in suspicion, and with his own hand deprived his child of life. And in like manner he cut off the head of his own daughter, so that all the gods were astonished at the disposition of Cronus.

But in process of time, whilst Ouranus was still in banishment, he sent his daughter Astarte, being a virgin, with two other of her sisters, Rhea and Dione, to cut off Cronus by treachery; but Cronus took the damsels, and married them notwithstanding they were his own sisters. When Ouranus understood this, he sent Eimarmene and Mora with other auxiliaries to make war against Cronus: but Cronus gained the affections of these also, and detained them with himself. Moreover, the god Ouranus devised Bætulia, contriving stones that moved as having life.

And by Astarte Cronus had seven daughters called Titanides, or Artemides; by Rhea also he had seven sons, the youngest of whom was consecrated from his birth; also by Dione he had daughters; and by Astarte again he had two other sons, Pothos and Eros.

And Dagon, after he had found out bread-corn, and the plough, was called Zeus Arotrius.

To Sydyc, who was called the just, one the Titanides bare Asclepius: and to Cronus there were born also in Peræa three sons, Cronus bearing the same name with his father, and Zeus Belus, and Apollo.

Contemporary with these were Pontus, and Typhon, and Nereus the father of Pontus: from Pontus descended Sidon, who by the excellence of her singing first invented the hymns of odes or praises: and Poseidon.

But to Demarous was born Melicarthus, who is also called Heracles.

Ouranus then made war against Pontus, but afterwards relinquishing the attack he attached himself to Demarous, when Demarous invaded Pontus: but Pontus put him to flight, and Demarous vowed a sacrifice for his escape.

In the thirty-second year of his power and reign, Ilus, who is Cronus, having laid an ambuscade for his father Ouranus in a certain place situated in the middle of the earth, when he had got him into his hands dismembered him over against the fountains and rivers. There Ouranus was consecrated, and his spirit was separated, and the blood of his parts flowed into the fountains and the waters of the rivers; and the place, which was the scene of this transaction, is shewed even to this day.

(Then our historian, after some other things, goes on thus:) But Astarte called the greatest, and Demarous named Zeus, and Adodus who is entitled the king of gods, reigned over the country by the consent of Cronus: and Astarte put upon her head, as the mark of her sovereignty, a bull's head: and travelling about the habitable world, she found a star falling through the air, which she took up, and consecrated in the holy island of Tyre: and the Phœnicians say that Astarte is the same as Aphrodite.

Moreover, Cronus visiting the different regions of habitable world, gave to his daughter Athena the kingdom of Attica: and when there happened a plague with a great mortality, Cronus offered up his only begotten son as a sacrifice to his father Ouranus, and circumcised himself, and compelled his allies to do the same: and not long afterwards he consecrated after his death another of his sons, called Muth, whom he had by Rhea; this (Muth) the Phœnicians esteem the same as Death and Pluto.

After these things, Cronus gave the city of Byblus to the goddess Baaltis, which is Dione, and Berytus to Poseidon, and to the Caberi who were husbandmen and fishermen: and they consecrated the remains of Pontus at Berytus.

But before these things the god Taautus, having pourtrayed Ouranus, represented also the countenances of the gods Cronus, and Dagon, and the sacred characters of the elements. He contrived also for Cronus the ensign of his royal power, having four eyes in the parts before and in the parts behind, two of them closing as in sleep; and upon the shoulders four wings, two in the act of flying, and two reposing as at rest. And the symbol was, that Cronus whilst he slept was watching, and reposed whilst he was awake. And in like manner with respect to the wings, that he was flying whilst he rested, yet rested whilst he flew. But for the other gods there were two wings only to each upon his shoulders, to intimate that they flew under the controul of Cronus; and there were also two wings upon the head, the one as a symbol of the intellectual part, the mind, and the other for the senses.

And Cronus visiting the country of the south, gave all Egypt to the god Taautus, that it might be his kingdom.

These things, says he, the Caberi, the seven sons of Sydyc, and their eighth brother Asclepius, first of all set down in the records in obedience to the commands of the god Taautus.

All these things the son of Thabion, the first Hierophant of all among the Phœnicians, allegorized and mixed up with the occurrences and accidents of nature and the world, and delivered to the priests and prophets, the superintendants of the mysteries: and they, perceiving the rage for these allegories increase, delivered them to their successors, and to foreigners: of whom one was Isiris, the inventor of the three letters, the brother of Chna who; is called the first Phœnician. — *Euseb. Præp. Evan.* lib. I. c. 10.

OF THE MYSTICAL SACRIFICE OF THE PHŒNICIANS.

It was the custom among the ancients, in times of great calamity, in order to prevent the ruin of all, for the rulers of the city or nation to sacrifice to the avenging deities the most beloved of their children as the price of redemption: they who were devoted this purpose were offered mystically. For Cronus, whom the Phœnicians call Il, and who after his death was deified and instated in the planet which bears his name, when king, had by a nymph of the country called Anobret an only son, who on that account is styled Ieoud, for so the Phœnicians still call an only son: and when great dangers from war beset the land he adorned the altar, and invested this son with the emblems of royalty, and sacrificed him. — *Euseb. Præp. Evan.* lib. I. c. 10. — lib. IV.

OF THE SERPENT.

Taautus first attributed something of the divine nature to the serpent and the serpent tribe; in which he was followed by the Phœnicians and Egyptians. For this animal was esteemed by him to be the most inspirited of all the reptiles, and of a fiery nature; inasmuch as it exhibits an incredible celerity, moving by its spirit without either hands, or feet, or any of those external members, by which other animals effect their motion. And in its progress it assumes a variety of forms, moving in a spiral course, and darting forward with whatever degree of swiftness it pleases. It is moreover long-lived, and has the quality not only of putting off its old age, and assuming a second youth, but of receiving at the same time an augmentation of its size and strength. And when it has fulfilled the appointed measure of its existence, it consumes itself; as Taautus has laid down in the sacred books; upon which account this animal is introduced in the sacred rites and mysteries. — *Euseb. Præp. Evan.* lib. I. c. 10.

FRAGMENTS
OF
CHALDÆAN HISTORY,
BEROSSUS:
FROM ALEXANDER POLYHISTOR.

OF THE COSMOGONY AND DELUGE.

BEROSSUS, in the first book of his history of Babylonia, informs us that he lived in the age of Alexander the son of Philip. And he mentions that there were written accounts, preserved at Babylon with the greatest care, comprehending a period of above fifteen myriads of years: and that these writings contained histories of the heaven and of the sea; of the birth of mankind; and of the kings, and of the memorable actions which they had achieved.

And in the first place he describes Babylonia as a country situated between the Tigris and the Euphrates: that it abounded with wheat, and barley, and ocrus, and sesame; and that in the lakes were produced the roots called gongre, which are fit for food, and in respect to nutriment similar to barley. That there were also palm trees and apples, and a variety of fruits; fish also and birds, both those which are merely of flight, and those which frequent the lakes. He adds, that those parts of the country which bordered upon Arabia, were without water, and barren; but that the parts which lay on the other side were both hilly and fertile.

At Babylon there was (in these times) a great resort of people of various nations, who inhabited Chaldæa, and lived in a lawless manner like the beasts of the field. In the first year there appeared, from that part of the Erythræan sea which borders upon Babylonia, an animal destitute[19] of reason, by name Oannes, whose whole body (according to the account of Apollodorus) was that of a fish; that under the fish's head he had another head, with feet also below, similar to those of a man, subjoined to the fish's tail. His voice too, and language, was articulate and human; and a representation of him is preserved even to this day.

This Being was accustomed to pass the day among men; but took no food at that season; and he gave them an insight into letters and sciences, and arts of every kind. He taught them to construct cities, to found temples, to compile laws, and explained to them the principles of geometrical knowledge. He made them distinguish the seeds of the earth, and shewed them how to collect the fruits; in short, he instructed them in every thing which could tend to soften manners and humanize their lives. From that time, nothing material has been added by way of improvement to his instructions. And when the sun had set, this Being Oannes, retired again into the sea, and passed the night in the deep; for he was amphibious. After this there appeared other animals like Oannes, of which Berossus proposes to give an account when he comes to the history of the kings. Moreover Oannes wrote concerning the generation of

---

[19] Endowed with Bry. — Terribilem feram Eu. Ar.

mankind; and of their civil polity; and the following is the purport of what he said:

"There was a time in which there existed nothing but darkness and an abyss of waters, wherein resided most hideous beings, which were produced of a two-fold principle. There appeared men, some of whom were furnished with two wings, others with four, and with two faces. They had one body but two heads: the one that of a man, the other of a woman: and likewise in their several organs both male and female. Other human figures were to be seen with the legs and horns of goats: some had horses' feet: while others united the hind quarters of a horse with the body of a man, resembling in shape the hippocentaurs. Bulls likewise were bred there with the heads of men; and dogs with fourfold bodies, terminated in their extremities with the tails of fishes: horses also with the heads of dogs: men too and other animals, with the heads and bodies of horses and the tails of fishes. In short, there were creatures in which were combined the limbs of every species of animals. In addition to these, fishes, reptiles, serpents, with other monstrous animals, which assumed each other's shape and countenance. Of all which were preserved delineations in the temple of Belus at Babylon.

The person, who presided over them, was a woman named Omoroca; which in the Chaldæan language is Thalatth;[20] in Greek Thalassa, the sea; but which might equally be interpreted the Moon. All things being in this situation, Belus came, and cut the

---

[20] Thalaatha Eu. Ar.

woman asunder: and of one half of her he formed the earth, and of the other half the heavens; and at the same time destroyed the animals within her.[21] All this (he says) was an allegorical description of nature. For, the whole universe consisting of moisture, and animals being continually generated therein, the deity above-mentioned took off his own head: upon which the other gods mixed the blood, as it gushed out, with the earth; and from thence were formed men. On this account it is that they are rational, and partake of divine knowledge. This Belus, by whom they signify Jupiter,[22] divided the darkness, and separated the Heavens from the Earth, and reduced universe to order. But the animals, not being able to bear the prevalence of light, died. Belus upon this, seeing a vast space unoccupied, though by nature fruitful, commanded one of the gods to take off his head, and to mix the blood with the earth; and from thence to form other men and animals, which should be capable of bearing the air.[23] Belus formed also the stars, and the sun, and the moon, and the five planets. (Such, according to Polyhistor Alexander, is the account which Berossus gives in his first book.)

(In the second book was contained the history of the ten kings of the Chaldæans, and the periods of the continuance of each reign, which consisted collectively of an hundred and twenty sari, or four hundred and thirty-two thousand years; reaching to

---

[21] "In the abyss." Bry. — "Which had composed her empire." Fab. — quæ in ipsa erant Eu. Ar.

[22] Dis Bry. — Dis or Pluto Fab. — Dios Eu. Ar.

[23] Light Bry.

the time of the Deluge. For Alexander, enumerating the kings from the writings of the Chaldæans, after the ninth Ardates, proceeds to the tenth, who is called by them Xisuthrus, in this manner:)

After the death of Ardates, his son Xisuthrus reigned eighteen sari. In his time happened a great Deluge; the history of which is thus described. The Deity, Cronus, appeared to him in a vision, and warned him that upon the fifteenth day of the month Dæsius there would be a flood, by which mankind would be destroyed. He therefore enjoined him to write a history of the beginning, procedure, and conclusion of all things; and to bury it in the city of the Sun at Sippara; and to build a vessel, and take with him into it his friends and relations; and to convey on board every thing necessary to sustain life, together with all the different animals; both birds and quadrupeds, and trust himself fearlessly to the deep. Having asked the Deity, whither he was to sail? he was answered,[24] "To the Gods:" upon which he offered up a prayer for the good of mankind. He then obeyed the divine admonition: and built a vessel five stadia in length, and two in breadth. Into this he put every thing which he had prepared; and last of all conveyed into it his wife, his children, and his friends.

After the flood had been upon the earth, and was in time abated, Xisuthrus sent out birds from the vessel; which, not finding any food, nor any place whereupon they might rest their feet, returned to him

---

[24] Roganti autem quo navigandum? Responsum; ad Deos, orandi causa, ut bona hominibus eveniant. Eu. Ar.

again. After an interval of some days, he sent them forth a second time; and they now returned with their feet tinged with mud. He made a trial a third time with these birds; but they returned to him no more: from whence he judged that the surface of the earth had appeared above the waters. He therefore made an opening in the vessel, and upon looking out found that it was stranded upon the side of some mountain; upon which he immediately quitted it with his wife, his daughter, and the pilot. Xisuthrus then paid his adoration to the earth: and having constructed an altar, offered sacrifices to the gods, and, with those who had come out of the vessel with him, disappeared.

They, who remained within, finding that their companions did not return, quitted the vessel with many lamentations, and called continually on the name of Xisuthrus. Him they saw no more; but they could distinguish his voice in the air, and could hear him admonish them to pay due regard to religion; and likewise informed them that it was upon account of his piety that he was translated to live with the gods; that his wife and daughter, and the pilot, had obtained the same honour. To this he added, that they should return to Babylonia; and, as it was ordained, search for the writings at Sippara, which they were to make known to all mankind: moreover that the place, wherein they then were, was the land of Armenia. The rest having heard these words, offered sacrifices to the gods; and taking a circuit, journeyed towards Babylonia.

The vessel being thus stranded in Armenia, some part of it yet remains in the Corcyræan[25] mountains of Armenia; and the people scrape off the bitumen, with which it had been outwardly coated, and make use of it by way of an alexipharmic and amulet. And when they returned to Babylon, and had found the writings at Sippara, they built cities, and erected temples: and Babylon was thus inhabited again. — *Syncel. Chron.* 28. — *Euseb. Chron.* 5. 8.

---

[25] or Codyèan Fab. — Corduarum montibus Eu. Ar.

BEROSSUS:
FROM APOLLODORUS.

OF THE CHALDÆAN KINGS.

THIS is the history which Berossus has transmitted to us. He tells us that the first king was Alorus of Babylon, a Chaldæan: he reigned ten sari: and afterwards Alaparus, and Amelon who came from Pantibiblon: then Ammenon the Chaldæan, in whose time appeared the Musarus Oannes the Annedotus from the Erythræan sea. (But Alexander Polyhistor anticipating the event, has said that he appeared in the first year; but Apollodorus says that it was after forty sari; Abydenus, however, makes the second Annedotus appear after twenty-six sari.) Then succeeded Megalarus from the city of Pantibiblon; and he reigned eighteen sari: and after him Daonus the shepherd from Pantibiblon reigned ten sari; in his time (he says) appeared again from the Erythræan sea a fourth Annedotus, having the same form with those above, the shape of a fish blended with that of a man. Then reigned Euedorachus from Pantibiblon, for the term of eighteen sari; in his days there appeared another personage from the Erythræan sea like the former, having the same complicated form between a fish and a man, whose name was Odacon. (All these, says Apollodorus, related particularly and circumstantially whatever Oannes had informed them of: concerning these Abydenus has made no mention.) Then reigned Amempsinus, a Chaldæan from Laranchæ: and he being the eighth in order reigned ten sari. Then reigned Otiartes, a Chaldæan, from Laranchæ; and he reigned eight sari. And upon the death of Otiartes, his son Xisuthrus reigned eighteen sari: in his time happened the great deluge. So that the sum of all the kings is ten; and the term which they collectively reigned an hundred and twenty sari. — *Syncel. Chron.* 39. — *Euseb. Chron.* 5.

BEROSSUS:
FROM ABYDENUS.

OF THE CHALDÆAN KINGS AND THE DELUGE.

So much concerning the wisdom of the Chaldæans.

It is said that the first king of the country was Alorus, and that he gave out a report that God had appointed him to be the Shepherd of the people: he reigned ten sari: now a sarus is esteemed to be three thousand six hundred years; a neros six hundred; and a sossus sixty.

After him Alaparus reigned three sari: to him succeeded Amillarus from the city of Pantibiblon, who reigned thirteen sari; in his time came up from the sea a second Annedotus, a semi-dæmon very similar in his form to Oannes: after Amillarus reigned Ammenon twelve sari, who was of the city of Pantibiblon: then Megalarus of the same place reigned eighteen sari: then Daos, the shepherd, governed for the space of ten sari; he was of Pantibiblon; in his time four double-shaped personages came up out of the sea to land, whose names were Euedocus, Eneugamus, Eneuboulus, and Anementus: afterwards in the time of Euedoreschus appeared another Anodaphus. After these reigned other kings, and last of all Sisithrus: so that in the whole, the number amounted to ten kings, and the term of their reigns to an hundred and twenty sari.

(And among other things not irrelative to the subject, he continues thus concerning the deluge:) After Euedoreschus some others reigned, and then Sisithrus. To him the deity Cronus foretold that on the fifteenth day of the month Desius there would be a deluge of rain: and he commanded him to deposit all the writings whatever which were in his possession, in the city of the Sun in Sippara. Sisithrus, when he had complied with commands, sailed immediately to Armenia, and was presently inspired by God. Upon the third day after the cessation of the rain Sisithrus sent out birds, by way of experiment, that he might judge whether the flood had subsided. But the birds passing over an unbounded sea, without finding any place of rest, returned again to Sisithrus. This he repeated with other birds. And when upon the third trial he succeeded, for the birds then returned with their feet stained with mud, the gods translated him from among men. With respect to the vessel, which yet remains in Armenia, it is a custom of the inhabitants to form bracelets and amulets of its wood. — *Syncel. Chron.* 38. — *Euseb. Præp. Evan.* lib. 9. — *Euseb. Chron.* 5. 8.

THE TOWER OF BABEL.

They say that the first inhabitants of the earth, glorying in their own strength and size, and despising the gods, undertook to raise a tower whose top should reach the sky, in the place in which Babylon now stands: but when it approached the heaven, the winds assisted the gods, and overthrew the work upon its contrivers: and its ruins are said to be still at Babylon: and the gods introduced a diversity of tongues among men, who till that time had all spoken the same language: and a war arose between Cronus and Titan. The place in which they built the tower is now called Babylon, on account of the confusion of the tongues; for confusion is by the Hebrews called Babel. — *Euseb. Præpe Evan.* lib. 9. — *Syncel. Chron.* 44. — *Euseb. Chron.* 13.

BEROSSUS:
FROM JOSEPHUS, &c.[26]

OF ABRAHAM.

AFTER the deluge, in the tenth generation, was a certain man among the Chaldæans renowned for his justice and great exploits, and for his skill in the celestial sciences. — *Euseb. Præp. Evan.* lib. 9.

OF NABONASAR.

From the reign of Nabonasar only are the Chaldæans (from whom the Greek mathematicians copy) accurately acquainted with the heavenly motions: for Nabonasar collected all the mementos of the kings prior to himself, and destroyed them, that the enumeration of the Chaldæan kings might commence with him. — *Syncel. Chron.* 207.

OF THE DESTRUCTION

OF THE JEWISH TEMPLE.

He (Nabopollasar) sent his son Nabuchodonosor with a great army against Egypt, and against Judea, upon his being informed that they had revolted from him; and by that means he subdued them all, and set

---

[26] The various readings to some of the following extracts would, if they were all given, exceed the text in size. I have selected those which appear to be most material.

fire to the temple that was at Jerusalem; and removed our people entirely out of their own country, and transferred them to Babylon, and our city remained in a state of desolation during the interval of seventy years, until the days of Cyrus king of Persia. (He then says, that) this Babylonian king conquered Egypt, and Syria, and Phœnicia, and Arabia, and exceeded in his exploits all that had reigned before him in Babylon and Chaldæa. — *Joseph. contr. Appion.* lib. 1. c. 19.

OF NEBUCHADNEZZAR.

When Nabopollasar his (Nabuchodnosor's) father, heard that the governor, whom he had set over Egypt, and the provinces of Cœlesyria and Phœnicia, had revolted, he was determined to punish his delinquencies, and for that purpose entrusted part of his army to his son Nabuchodonosor, who was then of mature age,[27] and sent him forth against the rebel: and Nabuchodonosor engaged and overcame him, and reduced the country again under his dominion. And it came to pass that his father, Nabopollasar, was seised with a disorder which proved fatal, and he died in the city of Babylon, after he had reigned nine and twenty years.

Nabuchodonosor, as soon as he had received intelligence of his father's death, set in order the affairs of Egypt and the other countries, and

------

[27] Lat. — Fab. — but a youth — Qy.

committed to some of his faithful officers the captives he had taken from the Jews, and Phœnicians, and Syrians, and the nations belonging to Egypt, that they might conduct them with that part of the forces which had heavy armour, together with the rest of his baggage, to Babylonia: in the mean time with a few attendants he hastily crossed the desert to Babylon. When he arrived there he found that his affairs had been faithfully conducted by the Chaldæans, and that the principal person among them had preserved the kingdom for him: and he acordingly obtained possession of all his father's dominions. And he distributed the captives in colonies in the most proper places of Babylonia: and adorned the temple of Belus, and the other temples, in a sumptuous and pious manner, out of the spoils which he had taken in this war. He also rebuilt the old city, and added another to it on the outside, and so far completed Babylon, that none, who might besiege it afterwards, should have it in their power to divert the river, so as to facilitate an entrance into it: and he effected this by building three walls about the inner city, and three about the outer. Some of these walls he built of burnt brick and bitumen, and some of brick only. When he had thus admirably fortified the city, and had magnificently adorned the gates, he added also a new palace to those in which his forefathers had dwelt, adjoining them, but exceeding them in height and splendor. Any attempt to describe it would be tedious: yet notwithstanding its prodigious size and magnificence it was finished within fifteen days. In this palace he erected very high walks, supported by stone pillars; and by planting what was called a pensile paradise, and replenishing it with all sorts of trees, he rendered the prospect an exact resemblance of a mountainous country. This he did to gratify his queen, because she had been brought up in Media, and was fond of a mountainous situation. — *Joseph. contr. Appion.* lib. 1. c. 19. — *Syncel. Chron.* 220. — *Euseb. Præp. Evan.* lib. 9.

OF THE CHALDÆAN KINGS AFTER NEBUCHADNEZZAR.

Nabuchodonosor, whilst he was engaged in building the above-mentioned wall, fell sick, and died after he had reigned forty-three years; whereupon his son Evilmerodachus succeeded him in his kingdom. His government however was conducted in an illegal and improper manner, and he fell a victim to a conspiracy which was formed against his life by Neriglissoorus, his sister's husband, after he had reigned about two years.

Upon his death Neriglissoorus, the chief of the conspirators, obtained possession of the kingdom, and reigned four years.

He was succeeded by his son Laborosoarchodus who was but a child, reigned nine months; for his misconduct he was seized by conspirators, and put to death by torture.

After his death, the conspirators assembled, and by common consent placed the crown upon the head of Nabonnedus, a man of Babylon, and one of the leaders of the insurrection. It was in his reign that the walls of the city of Babylon which defend the banks of the river were curiously built with burnt brick and bitumen.

In the seventeenth year of the reign of Nabonnedus, Cyrus came out of Persia with a great army, and having conquered all the rest of Asia, advanced hastily into the country of Babylonia. As soon as Nabonnedus perceived he was advancing to attack him, he assembled his forces and opposed him, but was defeated, and fled with a few of his adherents, and was shut up in the city of Borsippus. Upon this Cyrus took Babylon, and gave orders that the outer walls should be demolished, because the city appeared of such strength as to render a siege almost impracticable. From thence he marched to Borsippus, to besiege Nabonnedus: but Nabonnedus delivered himself into his hands without holding out the place: he was therefore kindly treated by Cyrus, who provided him with an establishment in Carmania, but sent him out of Babylonia. Nabonnedus accordingly spent the remainder of his life in that country, where he died. — *Joseph. contr. App.* lib. 1. c. 20. — *Euseb. Præp. Evan.* lib. 9.

OF THE FEAST OF SACEA.

Berossus, in the first book of his Babylonian history, says; That in the eleventh month, called Loos, is celebrated in Babylon the feast of Sacea for five days, in which it is the custom that the masters should obey their domestics, one of whom is led round the house, clothed in a royal garment, and him they call Zoganes. — *Athenæus*, lib. 14.

MEGASTHENES:
FROM ABYDENUS.

OF NEBUCHADNEZZAR.

ABYDENUS, in his history of the Assyrians, has preserved the following fragment of Megasthenes, who says: That Nabucodrosorus, having become more powerful than Hercules, invaded Libya and Iberia, and when he had rendered them tributary, he extended his conquests over the inhabitants of the shores upon the right of the sea. It is moreover related by the Chaldæans, that as he went up into his palace he was possessed by some god; and he cried out and said: "Oh! Babylonians, I, Nabucodrosorus, foretel unto you a calamity which must shortly come to pass, which neither Belus my ancestor, nor his queen Beltis, have power to persuade the Fates to turn away. A Persian mule shall come, and by the assistance of your gods shall impose upon you the yoke of slavery; the author of which shall be a Mede, the vain glory of Assyria. Before he should thus betray my subjects, Oh! that some sea or whirlpool might receive him, and his memory be blotted out for ever; or that he might be cast out to wander through some desert, where there are neither cities nor the trace of men, a solitary exile among rocks and caverns where beasts and birds alone abide. But for me, before he shall have conceived these mischiefs in his mind, a happier end will be provided."

When he had thus prophesied, he expired: and was suceeeded by his son Evilmaluruchus, who was slain by his kinsman Neriglisares: and Neriglisares left Labassoarascus his son: and when he also had suffered death by violence, they crowned Nabannidochus, who had no connexion with the royal family; and in his reign Cyrus took Babylon, and granted him a principality in Carmania.

And conceming the rebuilding of Babylon by Nabuchodonosor, he writes thus: It is said that from the beginning all things were water, called the sea: that Belus caused this state of things to cease, and appointed to each its proper place: and he surrounded Babylon with a wall: but in process of time this wall disappeared: and Nabuchodonosor walled it in again, and it remained so with its brazen gates until the time of the Macedonian conquest. And after other things he says: Nabuchodonosor having succeeded to the kingdom, built the walls of Babylon in a triple circuit in fifteen days; and he turned the river Armacale, a branch of the Euphrates, and the Acracanus: and above the city of Sippara he dug a receptacle for the waters, whose perimeter was forty parasangs, and whose depth was twenty cubits; and he placed gates at the entrance thereof, by opening which they irrigated the plains, and these they call Echetognomones (sluices): and he constructed dykes against the irruptions of the Erythræan sea, and built the city of Teredon to check the incursions of the Arabs; and he adorned the palaces with trees, calling them hanging gardens. — *Euseb. Præp. Evan.* lib. 10. — *Euseb. Chron.* 49.

SUPPLEMENTAL FRAGMENTS AND EXTRACTS ILLUSTRATIVE OF THE CHALDÆAN HISTORY.

OF THE ARK: FROM NICOLAUS DAMASCENUS.[28]

THERE is above Minyas in the land of Armenia a very great mountain which is called Baris;[29] to which, it is said, that many persons retreated at the time of the deluge, and were saved; and that one in particular was carried thither in an ark, and was landed on its summit, and that the remains of the vessel were long preserved upon the mountain. Perhaps this was the same individual of whom Moses the legislator of the Jews has made mention. — Jos. *Ant. Jud.* I. 3. — *Euseb. Præp. Evan.* 9.

OF THE DISPERSION: FROM HESTIÆUS.

THE priests who escaped took with them the implements of the worship of the Enyalian Jove, and

---

[28] Nicolaus Damascenus, a writer of Damascus about the age of Augustus. His fragments have been republished by Orellius. Leipzig.

[29] Baris signifies a ship. Walknaer's dissertation upon the word Baris may be found in the Preface to Valpy's edition of Stephans Thesaurus, p. 322. Epiphanius styles the mountain Lubar one of the mountains of Ararat; the Zendavesta calls it Albordi.

came to Senaar in Babylonia. But they were again driven from thence by the introduction of a diversity of tongues: upon which they founded colonies in various parts, each settling in such situations as chance or the direction of God led them to occupy. — *Jos. Ant. Jud.* I. c. 4. — *Euseb. Præp. Evan.* 9.

OF THE TOWER OF BABEL: FROM ALEXANDER POLYHISTOR.

THE Sibyl says: That when all men formerly spoke the same language; some among them undertook to erect a large and lofty tower, that they might climb up into heaven. But God[30] sending forth a whirlwind, confounded their design, and gave to each tribe a particular language of its own: which is the reason that the name of that city is Babylon. After the deluge lived Titan and Prometheus; when Titan undertook a war against Cronus.[31] — *Sync.* 44. — *Jos. Ant. Jud.* I. c. 4 — *Eus. Præp. Evan.* 9.

OF THE TOWER AND TITANIAN WAR: FROM THE SIBYLLINE ORACLES.[32]

---

[30] In the Armenian "Deus autem omnipotens," which agrees with the text of the Sibylline verses in the following page. Josephus and Eusebius have the plural ϑεοὶ, Gods.

[31] The last paragraph is not in the Greek copies, but the Armenian is as follows: — "Post diluvium autem Titan et Prometheus exstiterunt; ubi quidem Titan adversus Cronum (scil. Saturnum) bellum movebat."

[32] The translation is from the fourth volume of Bryant's Mythology, who has the following remarks upon the

BUT when the judgements of the Almighty God
Were ripe for execution; when the Tower
Rose to the skies upon Assyria's plain,
And all mankind one language only knew:
A dread commission from on high was given
To the fell whirlwinds, which with dire alarms
Beat on the Tower, and to its lowest base
Shook it convulsed. And now all intercourse,
By some occult and overruling power,
Ceased among men: by utterance they strove
Perplexed and anxious to disclose their mind;
But their lip failed them; and in lieu of words
Produced a painful babbling sound: the place
Was thence called Babel; by th' apostate crew
Named from the event. Then severed far away
They sped uncertain into the realms unknows:
Thus kingdoms rose; and the glad world was filled.

She then mentions Cronus, Titan and Jäpetus, and
the three sons of the patriarch governing the world in
the tenth generation after the deluge, thus,

---

fragment.—"It has been borrowed by some Hellenistic Jew, or
Gnostic, and inserted amid a deal of trash of his own composing.
The superior antiquity of that part which I have laid before the
reader, is plain from its being mentioned by Josephus. Some
lines are likewise quoted by Athenagoras, and Theophilus
Antiochenus. But there are passages afterwards which related to
circumstances of late date; such as were in time much inferior to
the age of Athenagoras; and still farther removed from the æra
of Josephus."

Καὶ τότε δὴ δεχάτη γενεὴ μερόπων ἀνϑρώπων,
Ἐξ οὗπερ χαταχλυσμὸς ἐπὶ προτέρους γένετ' ἄνδρας,
Καὶ βασίλευσε Κρόνος, χαὶ Τιτᾶν, Ἰαπετός τε,

The triple division of the earth is afterwards mentioned, over which each of the partriarchs ruled in peace.

Τρίσσαι δὴ μέριδες γαίης χατὰ χλῆρον ἐχάδτοῦ,
Καὶ βασίλευσεν ἔχαστος ἔχὼν μέρος, οὐδὲ μάχοντο

Then the death of Noah, and lastly the war between Cronus and Titan.

Καὶ μαχέσαντο Κρόνος Τιτᾶν τε πρὸς αὐτούς.

OF SCYTHISM AND HELLENISM
FROM EPIPHANIUS.[33]

The parents of all the heresies, and the prototypes from which they derive their names, and from which all other heresies originate, are these four primary ones.

The first is Barbarism,[34] which prevailed without a rival from the days of Adam through ten generations to the time of Noah. It is called Barbarism, because men had no rulers, nor submitted to any particular discipline of life; but as each thought proper to prescribe to himself; so he was at liberty to follow the dictates of his own inclination.

The second is Scythism which prevailed from the days of Noah and thence downwards to the building of the tower and Babylon, and for a few years subsequently to that time, that is to the days of Phalec and Ragau. But the nations which incline upon the borders of Europe continued addicted to the Scythic heresy, and the customs of the Scythians to the age of Thera, and afterwards; of this sect also were the Thracians.

The third is Hellenism, which originated in the days of Seruch with the introduction of idolatry: and as

---

[33] The following extract from Epiphanius is given also in the Paschal Chronicle in disjointed fragments. I have endeavoured to give the spirit of it as it may be gathered from a comparison of Epiphanius, Cedrenus and the Paschal Chronicle.

[34] Qy. Patriarchism?

men had hitherto followed each some demonolatrous superstition of his own, they were now reduced to a more established form of polity, and to the rites and ceremonies of idols. And the followers of this began with the use of painting, making likenesses of those whom they had formerly honoured, either kings or chiefs, or men who in their lives had performed actions which they deemed worthy of record, by strength or excellence of body.

The Egyptians, and Babylonians, and Phrygians, and Phœnicians were the first propagators of this superstition of making images, and of the mysteries: from whom it was transferred to the Greeks from the time of Cecrops downwards. But it was not till afterwards and at a considerable interval that Cronus and Rhea, Zeus and Apollo, and the rest were esteemed and honoured as gods.

The following extract is given in Epiphanius preceding the above.

AND from the times of Tharra the father of Abraham, they introduced images and all the errors of idolatry; honouring their forefathers, and their departed predecessors with effigies which they fashioned after their likeness. They first made these effigies of earthern ware, but afterwards according to their different arts they sculptured them in stone, and cast them in silver and gold, and wrought them in wood, and all kinds of different materials.

OF HELLENISM:
FROM CEDRENUS.

OF the tribe of Japhet was born Seruch, who first introduced Hellenism and the worship of idols. For he and those who concurred with him in opinion honoured their predecessors whether warriors or leaders, or characters renowned during their lives for valour or virtue with columnar statues, as if they had been their progenitors, and tendered to them a species of religious veneration as a kind of gods and sacrificed. But after this their successors, overstepping the intention of their ancestors that they should honour them as their progenitors and the inventors of good things with monuments alone, honoured them as heavenly gods and sacrificed to them as such. And the following was the form of their canonization: they inscribed their names after their decease in their sacred books and established a festival to each at certain seasons, saying that their souls had departed to the islands of the blessed and were never condemned or burnt with fire.

OF THE TOWER OF BABEL AND
ABRAHAM:
FROM EUPOLEMUS.

THE city of Babylon owes its foundation to those who were saved from the catastrophe of the deluge: they were the Giants, and they built the tower which is noticed in history. But the tower being overthrown by the interposition of God, the Giants were scattered over all the earth.

He says moreover that in the tenth generation in the city Camarina of Babylonia, which some call the city Urie, and which signifies a city of the Chaldæans, the thirteenth in descent lived Abraham, of a noble race, and superior to all others in wisdom; of whom they relate that he was the inventor of astrology and the Chaldæan magic, and that on account of his eminent piety he was esteemed by God. It is further said, that under the directions of God he removed and lived in Phœnicia, and there taught the Phœnicians the motions of the sun and moon and all other things; for which reason he was held in great reverence by their King. — *Euseb. Præp. Evan.* 9.

OF ABRAHAM:
FROM NICOLAUS DAMASCENUS.

ABRAM was king of Damascus, and he came thither as a stranger with an army from that part of the country which is situated above Babylon of the Chaldæans: but after a short time he again emigrated from this region with his people and transferred his habitation to the land, which was then called Cananæa, but now Judæa, together with all the multitude which had increased with him; of whose history I shall give an account in another book. The name of Abram is well-known even to this day in Damascus: and a village is pointed out which is still called the House of Abram. — *Euseb. Præp. Evan.* 9. — *Jos. Ant. Jud.* 1. 7.

OF BELUS:
FROM EUPOLEMUS.

FOR the Babylonians say that the first was Belus, who is the same as Cronus. And from him descended Belus and Chanaan; and this Chanaan was the father of the Phœnicians. Another of his sons was Chum, who is called by the Greeks Asbolus, father of the Ethiopians, and the father of Mestraim, the father of the Egyptians. The Greeks say, moreover, that Atlas was the discoverer of astrology. — *Eus. Pr. Ev.* lib. IX.

FROM THALLUS.

THALLUS makes mention of Belus, the king of the Assyrians, and Cronus the Titan; and says that Belus, with the Titans, made war against Zeus and his compeers, who are called Gods. He says, moreover, that Gygus was smitten, and fled to Tartessus.

According to the history of Thallus, Belus preceded the Trojan war 322 years. — *Theoph. ad Aut.* 281, 282.

OF THE ASSYRIAN EMPIRE:
FROM CTESIAS.

IN like manner all the other kings succeeded, the son receiving the empire from his father, being altogether thirty in their generations to Sardanapalus. In his time the empire passed to the Medes from the Assyrians, having remained with them upwards of

1360[35] years, according to the account of Ctesias the Cnidian, in his second book. — *Diod. Sic.* lib. II. p. 77.

FROM DIODORUS SICULUS.

IN the manner above related, the empire of the Assyrians, after having continued from Ninus thirty descents, and more than 1400 years, was finally dissolved by the Medes. — *Diod. Sic.* lib. II. p. 81.

FROM HERODOTUS.

THE Medes were the first who began the revolt from the Assyrians after they had maintained the dominion over Upper Asia for a period of 520 years. — *Lib.* I. c. 95.

OF NABOPOLASAR:
FROM ALEXANDER POLYHISTOR.[36]

NABOPOLASAR, whom Alexander Polyhistor calls Sardanapallus, sent to Astyages the Satrap of Media, and demanded his daughter Amuïtes in marriage for his son Nabuchodonosor. He was the commander of the army of Saracus King of the Chaldæans, and, having been sent upon some expedition, turned his arms against Saracus and marched against the city of Ninus (Nineveh). But Saracus confounded by his advance set fire to his palace and burnt himself in it. And Nabopolasar obtained the empire of the

---

[35] The Armenian omits the sixty years.
[36] This and the following fragments of Alexander Polyhistor are most probably extracts from the history of Berossus.

Chaldæans: he was the father of Nabuchodonosor. —
Euseb. Chron. 46.

OF THE CHALDÆAN AND ASSYRIAN KINGS:
FROM ALEXANDER POLYHISTOR.

IN addition to the above Polyhistor continues thus:
After the deluge Evexius held possession of the
country of the Chaldæans during a period of four
neri. And he was succeeded by his son Comosbelus,
who held the empire four neri and five sossi. But from
the time of Xisuthrus and the deluge, to that at which
the Medes took possession of Babylon, there were
altogether eighty-six kings. Polyhistor enumerates
and mentions each of them by name from the volume
of Berossus: the duration of the reigns of all which
kings comprehends a period of thirty-three thousand
and ninety-one years. But when their power was thus
firmly established, the Medes suddenly levied forces
against Babylon to surprise it, and to place upon the
throne kings chosen from among themselves.

He then gives the names of the Median Kings, 8 in
number, who reigned during the period of 224 years:
and again 11 Kings during . . . . years. Then 49 Kings
of the Chaldæans 458 years. Then 9 Kings of the
Arabians 245 years. After all these successive periods
of years he states that Semiramis reigned over the
Assyrians. And again minutely enumerates the names
of 45 Kings, assigning to them a term of 526 years.
After whom, he says there was a King of the
Chaldæans, whose name was Phulus: Of whom also

the historical writings of the Hebrews make mention under the name of Phulus (Pul) who they say invaded the country of the Jews. — *Eu. Ar. Chron.* 39.

OF SENECHERIB:
FROM ALEXANDER POLYHISTOR.

AFTER the reign of the brother of Senecherib, Acises reigned over the Babylonians, and when he had governed for the space of thirty days, he was slain by Marodach Baladanus, who held the empire by force during six months: and he was slain and succeeded by a person named Elibus. But in the third year of his reign Senecherib king of the Assyrians levied an army against the Babylonians; and in a battle, in which they were engaged, routed, and took him prisoner with his adherents, and commanded them to be carried into the land of the Assyrians. Having taken upon himself the government of the Babylonians, he appointed his son Asordanius their king, and he himself retired again into Assyria.

When he received a report that the Greeks had made a hostile descent upon Cilicia, he marched against them and fought with them a pitched battle, in which, though he suffered great loss in his own army, he overthrew them, and upon the spot he erected the statue of himself as a monument of his victory; and ordered his prowess to be inscribed upon it in the Chaldæan characters, to hand down the remembrance of it to posterity. He built also the city of Tarsus after the likeness of Babylon, which he called Tharsis. And after enumerating the various exploits of Sinnecherim, he adds that he reigned 18 years, and was cut off by a conspiracy which had been formed against his life by his son Ardumusanus. — *Eu. Ar. Chron.* 42.

OF SENECHERIB AND HIS SUCESSORS: FROM ALEXANDER POLYHISTOR.

AND after him (Pul) according to Polyhistor, Senecherib was king.

(The Chaldæan historian also makes mention of Senecherib himself, and Asordanus his son, and Marodach Baladanus, as well as Nabuchodonosorus.)

And Sinecherim reigned eighteen years; and after him his son eight years. Then reigned Sammuges twenty-one years, and likewise his brother twenty-one years. Then reigned Nabupalsar twenty years, and after him Nabucodrossorus forty-three years. (Therefore, from Sinecherim to Nabucodrossorus is comprehended a period altogether of eighty-eight years.)

After Samuges, Sardanapallus the Chaldæan, reigned twenty-one years. He sent an army to the assistance of Astyages the Mede, Prince and Satrap of the family, that he might give the Amuhean daughter of Astyages to his son Nabucodrossorus. Then reigned Nabucodrossorus forty-three years; and he came with a mighty army, and led the Jews, and Phœnicians, and Syrians into captivity.

And after Nabucodrorossus reigned his son Amilmarudochus, twelve years. . . . And after him Neglisarus reigned over the Chaldæans four years; and then Nabodenus seventeen years. In his reign Cyrus, the son of Cambyses, invaded the country of the Babylonians. Nabodenus went out to give him battle, but was defeated, and betook himself to flight: and Cyrus reigned at Babylon nine years. He was killed, however, in another battle, which took place in the plain of Daas. After him reigned Cambyses eight years; then Darius thirty-six years; after him Xerxes and the other kings of the Persian line. — *Eu. Ar. Chron.* pp. 41, 42. 44, 45.

OF SENECHERIB AND HIS SUCCESSORS: FROM ABYDENUS.

At the same time the twenty-fifth who was Senecherib can hardly be recognized among the kings. It was he who subjected the city of Babylon to his power, and defeated and sunk a Grecian fleet upon the coast of Cilicia. He built also a temple at Athens and erected brazen statues, upon which he engraved his own exploits. And he built the city of Tarsus after the plan and likeness of Babylon, that the river Cydnus should flow through Tarsus, in the same manner as the Euphrates intersected Babylon.

Next in order after him reigned Nergillus who was assassinated by his son Adramelus: and he also was slain by Axerdis (his brother by the same father, but of a different mother,) and his army pursued and blockaded in the city of Byzantium. Axerdis was the first that levied mercenary soldiers, one of whom was Pythagoras a follower of the wisdom of the Chaldæans: he also reduced under his dominion Egypt and the country of Cælo-Syria, whence came Sardanapallus.[37]

After him Saracus reigned over the Assyrians, and when he was informed that a very great multitude of barbarians had come up from the sea to attack him, he sent Busalossorus as his general in haste to Babylon. But he, having with a treasonable design obtained Amuhean, the daughter of Astyages the prince of the Medes, to be affianced to his son Nabuchodrossorus, marched straightways to surprise the city of Ninus, that is Nineveh. But when Saracus the king was apprized of all these proceedings he burnt the royal palace. And Nabuchodrossorus succeeded to the empire and surrounded Babylon with a strong wall. — *Eu. Ar. Chron.* 53.

OF BELUS AND THE ASSYRIAN EMPIRE: FROM CASTOR.

BELUS (says Castor) was king of the Assyrians; and under him the Cyclops assisted Jupiter with thunder-bolts and lightnings in his contest with the Titans. At that time there were kings of the Titans, one of whom was Ogygus. (After a short digression he proceeds to

---

[37] The name Sardanapallus is indiscriminately applied to various persons. Here perhaps Saracus may be intended; but from the fragment p. 59, most proably Busalossorus, i.e. Nabopolassar. The passage then in the text may refer to the dominion (potestatem) of Axerdis, "from which Sardanapallus revolted."

say, that) the Giants, in their attempted inroad upon the Gods, were slain by the assistance of Hercules and Dionysus, who were themselves of the Titan race.

Belus, whom we have mentioned above, after his death was esteemed a God. After him, Ninus reigned over the Assyrians fifty-two years. He married Semiramis, who, after his decease, reigned over the Assyrians forty-two years. Then reigned Zames, who is Ninyas. (Then he enumerates each of the successive Assyrian kings in order, and mentions them all, down to Sardanapallus, by their respective names: whose names, and the length of their reigns, we shall also give presently. Castor mentions them in his canon in the following words.)

We have first digested into a canon the kings of the Assyrians, commencing with Belus: but since we have no certain tradition respecting the length of his reign, we have merely set down his name, and commenced the chronological series from Ninus; and have concluded it with another Ninus, who obtained the empire after Sardanapallus; that in this manner the whole length of the time, as well as of the reigns of each king, might be plainly set forth. Thus it will be found, that the complete sum of the years amounts to 1280. — *Eus. Ar.* p. 81.

OF THE ASSYRIAN EMPIRE: FROM VELLEIUS AND AEMILIUS SURA.

THE Asiatic empire was subsequently transferred from the Assyrians, who had held it 1070 years, to the

Medes, from this time, for a period of 870 years. For Sardanapalus, the king of the Assyrians, a man wallowing in luxury, being the thirty-third from Ninus and Semiramis, the founders of Babylon, from whom the kingdom had passed in a regular descent from father to son, was deprived of his empire, and put to death by Arbaces the Mede. . . . . Æmilius Sura also, in his annals of the Roman people, says, "That the Assyrian princes extended their empire over all nations. They were succeeded by the Medes, then by the Persians, then by the Macedonians and shortly afterwards by two kings Philip and Antiochus, of Macedonian origin, who, not long after the destruction of Carthage, were conquered by the Romans, who then obtained the empire of the world. To this time, from the beginning of the reign of Ninus, king of the Assyrians, who first obtained the empire, there has elapsed a period of 1995 years." — *Hist. I. c. 6.*

OF THE CHALDÆAN OBSERVATIONS: FROM PLINIUS.

ANTICLIDES relates that they (letters) were invented in Egypt by a person whose name was Menon, fifteen years before Phoroneus the most ancient king of Greece: and he endeavours to prove it by the monuments. On the contrary, Epigenes, a writer of first-rate authority, informs us, that among the Babylonians were preserved observations of the stars, inscribed upon baked tiles, extending to a period of 720 years. Berosus and Critodemus, who are the most moderate in their calculations, nevertheless extend the period of the observations to 480 years. Whence may be inferred the eternal use of letters among them. — Lib. VII. c. 56.

FROM CICERO.

We must also contemn the Babylonians, and those who, in the region of Caucasus, pretend to have observed the heavens and courses of the stars: we must condemn them, I say, of folly, or of vanity, or of impudence, who assert that they have preserved upon monuments observations extending back during an interval of 470,000 years. — *De Divin.*

THE CHALDÆAN ORACLES OF ZOROASTER.

CAUSE
GOD, FATHER, MIND, FIRE MONAD,
DUAD, TRIAD.[38]

[38] Mr. Taylor in his collection of the oracles (Class. Journ. No. 22.) has arranged them under the following heads. I. The oracles which he conjectures may be ascribed to Zoroaster himself. This division includes the collection of Psellus, and in this collection are marked Z. as in the 8th. II. Oracles delivered by Theurgists under the reign of Marcus Antoninus. These relate to the Intelligible and Intellectual orders: and are here distinguished by a T as in the 4th. III. Oracles delivered either by the Theurgists or by Zoroaster, here marked Z or T. as in the 2nd. The rest he has placed together as uncertain or imperfect in their meaning; to which he has subjoined a few from the Treatise of Lydus de Mensibus. We are also indebted to Mr. Taylor for the references to the authors from whom the collection was originally made, and for the addition of several oracles hitherto unnoticed: the latter are distinguished by the letters *Tay.* after the reference, as in the 2nd oracle.

1.[39]   But God is he that has the head of a hawk. He is
the first, indestructible, eternal, unbegotten,
indivisible, dissimilar; the dispenser of all good;
incorruptible; the best of the good, the wisest of the
wise: he is the father of equity and justice, self-
taught, physical, and perfect, and wise, and the
only inventor of the sacred philosophy.

Euseb. Præp. Evan. lib. I. c. 10.

2.[40]   Theurgists assert that he[41] is a God, and celebrate
him as both older and younger, as a circulating and
eternal God, as understanding the whole number
of all things moved in the world, and moreover
infinite through his power and of a spiral form.

Z. or T.   *Proc. in Tim.* 244. — *Tay.*

3.   The mundane god, eternal, boundless,
Young and old, of a spiral form.

---

[39] Eusebius attributes this to the Persian Zoroaster. I have added
it to the collection.

[40] Lobeck seems to be of opinion that neither this nor the one
next following have any claim to be inserted.

[41] χϑόνος, Time Tay. — Qy. Κρόνος. The latter Platonists
continually substitute Χρόνος for Κϑόνος.

4.   For Eternity,[42] according to the oracle, is the cause
        of never-failing life, of unwearied power, and
        unsluggish energy.

        T.   *Tay.*

5.   Hence this stable God is called by the gods silent,
        and is said to consent with mind, and to be known
        by souls through mind alone.

        T.   *Proc. in Theol. 321. — Tay.*

6.   The Chaldæans call the God (Dionysus or Bacchus)
        Iao in the Phœnician tongue (instead of the
        intelligible light), and he is often called Sabaoth,
        signifying that he is above the seven poles, that is
        the Demiurgus.

                            Lyd. de Mens. 83. — Tay.

7.   Containing all things in the one summit of his own
        hyparxis, he himself subsists wholly beyond.

        T.   *Procl. in Theol. 212. — Tay.*

---

[42] The Gnostics used the word Æon itself for their different
celestial orders. See also Sanchoniatho. p. 4.

8.   Measuring and bounding all things.

        T.   *Proc. in Pl. Th.* 386. — *Tay.*

9.   For nothing imperfect circulates from a paternal principle.

        Z.   *Psell.* 38. — *Plet.*

10.   The father hurled not forth fear but infused persuasion.

        Z.   *Plet.*

11.   . . . . The Father has hastily withdrawn himself;
        But has not shut up his own fire in his intellectual power.

        Z.   *Psell.* 30. — *Plet.* 33.

12.   Such is the Mind which is there energizing before energy.

That it has not gone forth but abode in the paternal
depth,
And in the adytum according to divinely-
nourished silence.

    T.   *Proc. in Tim.* 167.

13.   All things are the progeny of one fire.
The Father perfected all things, and delivered them
over
To the second Mind, whom all nations of men call
the first.

    Z.   *Psell.* 24. — *Plet.* 30.

14.   And of the Mind which conducts the empyrean
world.

    T.   *Dam. de Prin.*

15.   What the Mind says, it says by understanding.

    Z.   *Psell.* 35.

16.   Power is with them, but Mind is from him.

17.   The Mind of the Father riding on attenuated rulers
           Which glitter with the furrows of inflexible and
           implacable Fire.

           T.   *Proc. in Crat. — Tay.*

18.   . . . . . . After the paternal conception
           I the Soul reside, a heat animating all things.
           . . . . . . For he placed
           Mind in Soul and Soul in dull Body,
           The Father of Gods and Men so placed them in
           ours.

           Z. or T.   *Proc. in Tim.* 124.

19.   Natural works coexist with the intellectual light
           Of the Father. For it is the Soul, which adorned the
           great heaven
           And which adorns it after the Father.
           But her horns are established on high.

           Z. or T.   *Proc. in Tim.* 106.

20.   The Soul, being a bright fire, by the power of the father,
      Remains immortal, and is mistress of life,
      And fills up many of the recesses of the world.

      Z.   *Psell.* 28. — *Plet.* 11.

21.   The channels being intermixed, she performs the works of incorruptible fire.

      Z. or T.   *Proc. in Pl. Polit.* 399.

22.   For the Fire which is first beyond did not shut up his power
      In matter by works but by mind:
      For the framer of the fiery world is the Mind of Mind.

      T.   *Proc. in Theol.* 333. — *in Tim.* 157.

23.   Who first sprung from Mind
      Clothing fire with fire, binding them together that he might mingle
      The fountainous craters, while he preserved the flower of his own fire.

      T.   *Proc. in Parm.*

24.   Thence a fiery whirlwind drawing the flower of
     glowing fire,
     Flashing into the cavities of the worlds; for all
     things from thence
     Begin to extend downwards their admirable rays.

     T.   *Proc. in Theol. Plat.* 171. 172.

25.[43]   The Monad is there first where the paternal Monad
     subsists.

     T.   *Proc. in Euc.* 27.

26.   The Monad is extended which generates two.

     T.   *Proc. in Euc.* 27.

27.   For the Duad sits by this, and glitters with
     intellectual sections,
     To govern all things, and to order each.

---

[43] What the Pythagoreans signify by Monad, Duad, and Triad —
or Plato by Bound, Infinite, or Mixed; or we in the former part of
this work, by The One, The Many, and The United; that the
oracles of the Gods intend by Hyparxis, Power, and Energy. —
Dam. de Prin. — *Tay.*

T.   *Proc. in Plat.* 376.

28.   The Mind of the Father said that all things should
       be cut into three:
       His will assented, and immediately all things were
       cut.

       T.   *Proc. in Parm.*

29.   The Mind of the eternal Father said into three,
       Governing all things by Mind,

       T.   *Proc. in Tim.*

30.   The Father mingled every Spirit from this Triad.

                    Lyd. de Men. 20.—*Tay.*

31.   All things are governed in the bosoms of this triad.

                    Lyd. de Men. 20.—*Tay.*

113

32.   All things are governed and subsist in these three.

       T.   *Proc. in I. Alcib.*

33.   For you may conceive that all things serve these three principles.

       T.   *Dam. de Prin.*

34.   From these flows the body of the Triad, being pre-existent,
Not the first, but that by which things are measured.

       Z. or T.   *Anon.*

35.   And there appeared in it virtue, and wisdom,
And multiscient truth.

       Z. or T.   *Anon.*

36.   For in the whole world shineth a Triad, over which a Monad rules.

T.   Dam. in Parm.

37.   The first is the sacred course . . . . , but in the middle
           Air, the third the other which cherisheth the earth in fire.

               Z. or T.   Anon.

38.   Abundantly animating light, fire, ether, worlds.

               Z. or T.   Simp. in Phys. 143.

IDEAS[44]
INTELLIGIBLES, INTELLECTUALS,

[44] The whole of the following division is a system grafted upon the Platonic doctrine of Ideas. It is composed of six different orders, called Triads, or each consisting of three Triads, which have different names in the respective theologies of the Modern Platonists, and of those who assumed the title of Chaldæans. Both regarded the first Cause as the One and the Good; from whom proceeded in succession the three first orders which were all Ineffable and Superessential.

I. The first Order is the *Intelligible Triad* of the Platonists, but Psellus says it was venerated among the Chaldæans as a *certain Paternal Profundity*, containing three triads, each consisting of Father, Power and Intellect.

II. The second order of the Platonists was the *Intelligible and at the same time Intellectual Triad*. Among the Chaldæans it consisted of the *Iynges, Syonches and Teletarchæ.*

III. The *Intellectual Triad* of later Platonists corresponds with the *Fountains or Fontal Fathers* of the Chaldæans.

The last of the Intellectual Triad was the Demiurgus, from whom proceeded the Effable and Essential orders including all sorts of Dæmons. They are according to the respective systems —

OF THE PLATONISTS.	OF THE CHALDEANS.
IV. The Supermundane.	IV. The Principles.
V. The Liberated.	V. The Azonic.
VI. The Mundane.	VI. The Zonic.

116

IYNGES, SYNOCHES, TELETARCHÆ, FOUNTAINS, PRINCIPLES, HECATE AND DÆMONS.

The Mind of the Father made a jarring noise,
understanding by unwearied counsel
Omniform ideas: which flying out from one
fountain
They sprung forth: for from the Father was the
will and the end;

(By which they are connected with the Father
According to alternate life from several vehicles,)
But they were divided, being by intellectual fire
distributed
Into other Intellectuals: For the king previously
placed before the multiform world

An intellectual, incorruptible pattern, the print of
whose form

Is promoted through the world, according to
which things the world appeared
Beautified with all-various Ideas; of which there is
one fountain,

The Demiurgus was the fabricator of the world, and held the same relative position to the three succeeding essential orders as did the first cause to the three preceding or superessential orders.

From this the others rush forth distributed,
And separated about the bodies of the world, and
are borne

Through its vast recesses like swarms
Turning themselves on all sides in every direction,
They are Intellectual conceptions from the
paternal fountain,

Partaking abundantly the flower of Fire in the
point of restless time,

But the primary self-perfect fountain of the Father
Poured forth these primogenial ideas.

Z. or T. *Proc. in Parm.*

These being many ascend flashingly into the
shining worlds
And in them are contained three summits.

T. *Dam. in Parm.*

They are the guardians of the works of the Father
And of the one Mind, the Intelligible.

T. *Proc. in Th. Plat.* 205.

All things subsist together in the Intelligible world.

T.   *Dam. de Prin. — Tay.*

But all Intellect understands the deity, for Intellect is not without the Intelligible,

And the Intelligible does not subsist apart from Intellect.

Z. or T.   *Dam.*

For Intellect is not without the Intelligible: it does not subsist apart from it.

Z. or T.   *Proc. Th. Plat.* 172.

By Intellect he contains the Intelligibles, but introduces the Soul into the worlds.

By Intellect he contains the Intelligibles, but introduces Sense into the worlds.

T.   *Proc. in Crat.*

119

For the paternal Intellect, which understands Intelligibles,
And adorns things ineffable, has sowed symbols through the world.

T.   *Proc. in Crat.*

This order is the beginning of all section.

T.   *Dam. de Prin.*

The Intelligible is the principle of all section.

T.   *Dam. de Prin.*

The Intelligible is food to that which understands.

T.   *Dam. de Prin.*

The oracles concerning the orders exhibits it prior to Heaven as ineffable, and add —

It has mystic silence.

T. *Proc. in Crat. — Tay.*

The oracle calls the Intelligible causes Swift, and asserts that proceeding from the Father, they run to him.

T. *Proc. in Crat. — Tay.*

Those natures are both Intellectual and Intelligible, which, themselves possessing intellection, are the objects of intelligence to others.

T. *Proc. Th. Plat. 179.*

The intelligible Iynges themselves understand from the Father;
By ineffable counsels being moved so as to understand.

Z. *Psell. 41. — Plet. 31..*

Because it is the operator, because it is the giver of

life-bearing fire.
Because it fills the life-producing bosom of
Hecate.
And it instils into the Synoches the enlivening
strength of Fire
Endued with mighty power.

T.   *Proc. in Tim.* 128.

He gave to his own whirlwinds to guard the
summits,
Mingling the proper force of his own strength in
the Synoches.

T.   *Dam. de Prin.*

But likewise as many as serve the material
Synoches.

T.

The Teletarchs are comprehended in the
Synoches.

T.   *Dam. de Prin.*

Rhea the fountain and river of the blessed
Intellectuals
Having first received the powers of all things in
her ineffable bosom
Pours forth perpetual generation upon every
thing.

T.   *Proc. in Crat. — Tay.*

For it is the bound of the paternal depth, and the
fountain of the Intellectuals.

T.   *Dam. de Prin.*

. . . . For he is a power
Of circumlucid strength, glittering with
Intellectual sections.

T.   *Dam.*

He glitters with Intellectual sections, but has filled
all things with love.

T.   *Dam.*

To the Intellectual whirlwinds of Intellectual fire all things

Are subservient, through the persuasive counsel of the Father.

T.   *Proc. in Parm.*

Oh how the world has inflexible Intellectual rulers.

The centre of Hecate corresponds with that of the fathers.

T.

From him leap forth all implacable thunders,
And the whirlwind receiving bosoms of the all-splendid strength

Of the Father-begotten Hecate; and he who begirds the flower of fire

And the strong spirit of the poles, all fiery beyond.

T.   *Proc. in Crat.*

Another fontal, which leads the empyreal world.

Z. or T.   *Proc. in Tim.*

The fountain of fountains, and the boundary of all fountains.

T.   *Dam. de Prin.*

Under two minds the life-generating fountain of souls is comprehended.

T.   *Dam. de Prin.*

Beneath them lies the principal of the immaterials.

Z. or T.   *Dam. in Parm.*

Father-begotten light, for he alone having
gathered from the strength of the Father
The flower of mind has the power of
understanding, the paternal mind;

To instil into all fountains and principles the
power
Of understanding, and of always remaining in a
ceaseless revolution,

T.   *Proc. in Tim.* 242.

All fountains and principles whirl round,
And always remain in a ceaseless revolution.

Z. or T.   *Proc. in Parm.*

The Principles, which have understood the
Intelligible works of the Father
He has clothed in sensible works and bodies,
Being the intermediate links standing to
communicate between the Father and Matter,
Rendering apparent the images of unapparent
natures,
And inscribing the unapparent in the apparent
frame of the world.

Z. or T.   *Dam. de Prin.*

Typhon, Echidna, and Python, being the progeny
of Tartarus and Earth, which is conjoined with
Heaven, form as it were a certain Chaldaic triad,

which is the inspector of the whole disordered
fabrication.

T.   *Olymp in Phæd. — Tay.*

Irrational dæmons derive their subsistence from
the aërial rulers, wherefore the oracle says,
Being the charioteer of the aërial, terrestrial, and
aquatic dogs.

T.   *Olymp. in Phæd. — Tay.*

The aquatic, when applied to divine natures,
signifies a government inseparable from water,
and hence the oracle calls the aquatic gods water
walkers.

T.   *Proc. in Tim. 270. — Tay.*

There are certain aquatic dæmons whom Orpheus
called Nereides in the more elevated exhalations
of water such as appear in this cloudy air, whose
bodies are sometimes seen, as Zoroaster thinks, by
more acute eyes, especially in Persia and Africa.

T.   *Fic. de Im. Am. 123. — Tay.*

PARTICULAR SOULS.
SOUL, LIFE, MAN.

These things the Father conceived, and the
8.   mortal was animated for him.

T.   *Proc. in Tim.* 336.

For the Father of gods and men placed the mind
9.   in soul,
But in body he placed you.

The paternal mind has sowed symbols in the
0.   souls.

Z.   *Psell.* 26 — *Plet.* 6.

1. Having mingled the vital spark from two according substances,
Mind and Divine Spirit, as a third to these he added
Holy Love, the venerable charioteer uniting all things.

Lyd. de Men. 3. — *Tay.*

2. Filling the soul with profound love.

Z. or
T.
Proc. in Pl. Theol. 4.

3. The Soul of men will in a manner clasp God to herself.
Having nothing mortal she is wholly inebriated from God,
For she glories in the harmony under which the mortal body exists.

Z.
Psell. 17. — *Plet.* 10.

The more powerful souls perceive truth through

4.   themselves, and are of a more inventive nature. "Such souls are saved through their own strength," according to the oracle.

T.   *Proc. in I. Alc. — Tay.*

5.   The oracle says, ascending souls sing a pæan.

Z. or
T.   *Olym. in Phæd. — Tay.*

6.   Of all souls those certainly are superlatively blessed
Which are poured forth from heaven to earth;
And they are happy, and have ineffable stamina,
As many as proceed from thy splendid self, O king,
Or from Jove himself, under the strong necessity of Mithus.

Z. or
T.   *Synes de Insom.* 153.

The souls of those who quit the body violently

7.   are most pure.

         Z.   *Psel.* 27.

        The ungirders of the soul, which give her

8.   breathing, are easy to be loosed.

         Z.   *Psel.* 32. — *Plet.* 8.

        For tho' you see this soul manumitted

9.   The Father sends another, that the number may be
complete.

         Z. or

T.

        . . . . . Understanding the works of the Father

0.   They avoid the shameless wing of fate;
They are placed in God, drawing strong torches,
Descending from the Father, from which, as they
descend, the soul
Gathers of the empyreal fruits the soul-nourishing
flower.

Z. or
T.

Proc in Tim. 321.

1.   This animastic spirit, which blessed men have called the pneumatic soul, becomes a god, an all-various dæmon, and an image, and the soul in this suffers her punishments. The oracles, too, accord with this account: for they assimilate the employment of the soul in Hades to the delusive visions of a dream.

Z. or
T.

Synes. de Insom. p. 139. — *Tay.*

2.   One life with another, from the distributed channels.
Passing from above through the opposite part
Through the centre of the earth; and the fifth the middle,
Another fiery channel, where the life-beaming fire descends
As far as the material channels.

Z. or
T.

3.
Moisture is a symbol of life; hence Plato, and the gods before Plato, call it (the soul); at one time the liquid of the whole of vivification, and at another time a certain fountain of it.

Z. *Proc. in Tim.* 318. — *Tay.*

4.
O man, of a daring nature, thou subtile production.

Z. *Psel.* 12. — *Plet.* 21.

5.
For thy vessel the beasts of the earth shall inhabit.

Z. *Psel.* 36.-*Plet.* 7.

6.
Since the soul perpetually runs and passes through all things in a certain space of time, which being performed, it is presently compelled to run back again through all things and unfold the same web of generation in the world, according to

Zoroaster, who thinks that as often as the same causes return, the same effects will in like manner be returned.

Z.   *Ficin de Im. An.* 129. — *Tay.*

7.   According to Zoroaster, in us the ethereal vestment of the soul perpetually revolves.

Z.   *Ficin de Im. An.* 131. — *Tay.*

8.   The oracles delivered by the gods celebrate the essential fountain of every soul, the empyrean, the etherial, and the material. This fountain they separate from the whole vivific goddess[12]; from whom also suspending the whole of fate, they make two series, the one animastic, or belonging to the soul, and the other belonging to Fate. They assert that the soul is derived from the animastic series, but that sometimes it becomes subservient to Fate, when passing into an irrational condition of being, it becomes subject to fate instead of Providence.

Z. or   *Proc. de Prov. ap. Fabr. VIII.* 486. —
T.   *Tay.*

MATTER.
MATTER, THE WORLD, AND NATURE.

99.   The matrix containing all things.

          T.

100.   Wholly division, and indivisible.

101.   Thence abundantly springs forth the generation of
          multifarious matter.

          T.   *Proc. in Tim.* 118.

102.   These frame indivisibles and sensibles,
          And corporiforms and things destined to matter.

          T.   *Dam. de Prin.*

103.   The fontal nymphs, and all the aquatic spirits,
And the terrestrial, aerial, and glittering recesses,
Are the lunar riders and rulers of all matter,
Of the celestial, the starry, and that which lies in
the abysses.

Lyd. p. 32. — *Tay.*

104.   Evil, according to the oracle, is more frail than
nonentity.

Z. or T.   *Proc. de Prov.* — *Tay.*

105.   We learn that matter pervades the whole world,
as the gods also assert.

Z. or T.   *Proc. Tim.* 142.

106.   All divine natures are incorporeal,
But bodies are bound in them for your sakes.
Bodies not being able to contain incorporeals
By reason of the corporeal nature, in which you
are concentrated.

Z. or T.   *Proc. in Pl. Polit.* 359.

107. For the paternal self-begotten mind
      understanding his works
      Sowed in all the fiery bond of love,
      That all things might continue loving for an
      infinite time.
      That the connected series of things might
      intellectually remain in all the light of the Father,
      That the elements of the world might continue
      their course in love.

      T.   *Proc. in Tim.* 155.

108. The Maker who, self-operating, framed the world,
      And there was another mass of fire: all these
      things
      He produced self-operating, that the body of the
      world might be conglobed,
      That the world might be manifest, and not appear
      membranous.

      Z. or T.   *Proc. in Tim.* 154.

109. For he assimilates himself, professing
      To cast around him the form of the images.

110.   For it is an imitation of Mind, but that which is fabricated has something of body.

        Z. or T.   *Proc .in Tim.* 87.

111.   But projecting into the worlds, through the rapid menace of the Father,
The venerable name with a sleepless revolution.

        Z. or T.   *Proc. in Crat.*

112.   The ethers of the elements therefore are there.

        Z. or T.   *Olymp. in Phæd. — Tay.*

113.   The oracles assert, that the impression of characters, and of other divine visions, appear in the ether.

        Z. or T.   *Simp. in Phys.* 144. — *Tay.*

114.   In this the things without figure are figured.

        Z. or T.   *Simp. in Phys.* 143.

115.   The ineffable and effable impressions of the
         world.

116.   And the light-hating world, and the winding
         currents
         Under which many are drawn down.

         Z. or T.   *Proc. in Tim.* 339.

117.   He makes the whole world of fire, and water, and
         earth,
         And all-nourishing ether.

         Z. or T.

118.   Placing earth in the middle, but water in the
         cavities of the earth,
         And air above these.

         Z. or T.

119.   He fixed a great multitude of inerratic stars,
         Not by a laborious and evil tension,

But with a stability void of wandering.
Forcing the fire to the fire.

  Z. or T. *Proc. in Tim.* 280.

120. For the Father congregated the seven firmaments
    of the world,
    Circumscribing the heavan with a convex figure.

  Z. or T. *Dam. in Parm.*

121. He constituted a septenary of erratic animals.

  Z. or T.

122. Suspending their disorder in well-disposed zones.

  Z. or T.

123. He made them six in number, and for the seventh
    He cast into the midst the fire of the sun.

  Z. or T. *Proc. in Tim.* 280.

124.   The centre from which all (lines) which way so ever are equal.

   Z. or T.   *Proc. in Euc.* 43.

125.   And that the swift sun may come as usual about the centre.

   Z. or T.   *Proc. in Plat. Th.* 317.

126.   Eagerly urging itself towards the centre of resounding light.

   T.   *Proc. in Tim.* 236.

127.   And the great sun and the bright moon.

128.   For his hairs appear like rays of light ending in a sharp point.

   T.   *Proc. in Pl. Pol.* 387.

129. And of the solar circles, and of the lunar clashings,
And of the aerial recesses,
The melody of the ether, and of the sun, and of the passages of the moon, and of the air.

Z. or T.   *Proc. in Tim. 257.*

130. The most mystic of discourses inform us, that the wholeness of him (the sun) is in the supermundane orders: for there a solar world and a total light subsist, as the oracles of the Chaldæans affirm.

Z. or T.   *Proc. in Tim. 264. — Tay.*

131. The more true sun measures all things by time, being truly a time of time, according to the oracle of the gods concerning it.

Z. or T.   *Proc. in Tim. 249. — Tay.*

132. The disk (of the sun) is carried in the starless much above the inerratic sphere: and hence he is not in the middle of the planets but of the three

worlds, according to the telestic hypotheses

Z. or T.   *Jul. Orat. V. 334. — Tay.*

133.   (The sun is a)13 fire, the channel of fire, and the dispenser of fire.

Z. or T.   *Proc. in Tim. 141.*

134.14   Hence Cronus.
The sun assessor beholding the pure pole.

135.   The ethereal course and the vast motion of the moon
And the aerial fluxes.

Z. or T.   *Proc. in Tim. 257.*

136.   Oh ether, sun, spirit of the moon, leaders of the air.

Z. or T.   *Proc. in Tim. 257.*

137. And the wide air, and the lunar course, and the
pole of the sun.

Z. or T.   *Proc. in Tim.* 257.

138. For the goddess brings forth the great sun and the
bright moon.

139. She collects it, receiving the melody of the ether,
And of the sun, and of the moon, and of
whatsoever things are contained in the air.

140. Unwearied nature rules over the worlds and
works,
That heaven drawing downward might run an
eternal course,
And that the other periods of the sun, moon,
seasons, night, and day, might be accomplished.

Z. or T.   *Proc. in Tim.* 4. & 323. — *Tay.*

141. Immense nature is exalted about the shoulders of
the goddess.

T.   *Proc. in Tim.* 4.

142.   The most celebrated of the Babylonians, together with Ostanes and Zoroaster, very properly call the starry spheres *herds*; whether because these alone among corporeal magnitudes, are perfectly carried about a centre, or in conformity to the oracles, because they are considered by them as in a certain respect the bonds and collectors of physical reasons, which they likewise call in their sacred discourses herds, and by the insertion of a *gamma*, angels. Wherefore the stars which preside over each of these herds are considered demons similar to the angels, and are called archangels: and they are seven in number.

Z.   *Anon. in Theologumenis*
            Arithmeticis. — Tay.

143.   Zoroaster calls the congruities of material forms to the reasons of the soul of the world, divine allurements.

Z.   *Fic. de vit. cœl. comp. 519. — Tay.*

MAGICAL AND PHILOSOPHICAL PRECEPTS.

144.   Direct not thy mind to the vast measures of the
earth;
For the plant of truth is not upon ground.
Nor measure the measures of the sun, collecting
rules,
For he is carried by the eternal will of the father,
not for your sake.
Dismiss the impetuous course of the moon; for
she runs always by the work of necessity.
The progression of the stars was not generated for
your sake.
The wide aerial flight of birds is not true,
Nor the dissections of the entrails of victims: they
are all mere toys,
The basis of mercenary fraud: flee from these
If you would open the sacred paradise of piety
Where virtue, wisdom, and equity, are assembled.

      Z.   *Psel.* 4.

145.   Stoop not down to the darkly-splendid world;
In which continually lies a faithless depth, and
Hades
Cloudy, squalid, delighting in images
unintelligible,
Precipitous, winding, a blind profundity always
rolling,

Always espousing an opacous, idle, breathless body.

Z. or T.   *Synes de Insom.* 140.

146.   Stoop not down, for a precipice lies below the
        earth,
        Drawing under a descent of seven steps, beneath
        which
        Is the throne of dire necessity.

        Z.   *Psel.* 6 — *Plet.* 2.

147.   Leave not the dross of matter on a precipice,
        For there is a portion for the image in a place ever
        splendid.

        Z.   *Psel.* 1. 2. — *Plet.* 14. — *Syn.* 140.

148.   Invoke not the self-conspicuous image of nature.

        Z.   *Psel.* 15. — *Plet.* 23.

149.   Look not upon nature, for her name is fatal.

Z.   *Proc. in Plat. Th.* 143.

150.   It becomes you not to behold them before your
body is initiated,
Since by always alluring, they seduce the souls of
the initiated.

      Z. or T.   *Proc. in. Alcib.*

151.   Bring her[15] not forth, lest in departing she retain
something.

      Z.   *Psel.* 3. — *Plet.* 15.

152.   Defile not the spirit, nor deepen a superficies.

      Z.   *Psel.* 19. — *Plet.* 13.

153.   Enlarge not thy destiny.

      Z.   *Psel.* 37. — *Plet.* 4.

154.   Not hurling, according to the oracle, a
transcendent foot towards piety.

      Z. or T.   *Dam. in vit. Isidori ap. Suid. — Tay.*

155.   Never change barbarous names,
For there are names in every nation given from
God,
Having unspeakable efficacy in the mysteries.

      Z. or T.   *Psel. 7. — Niceph.*

156.   Go not out when the lictor passes by.

      Z.   *Pic. Concl. — Tay.*

157.   Let fiery hope nourish you in the angelic region.

      Z. or T.   *Olym. in Phæd. — Proc. in Alcib.*

158.   The fire-glowing conception has the first rank,
For the mortal who approaches the fire shall have
light from God,
For to the persevering mortal, the blessed
immortals are swift.

Z. or T.   *Proc. in Tim.* 65.

159.   The Gods exhort us
            To understand the preceding form of light.

            Z. or T.   *Proc. in Crat. — Tay.*

160.   It becomes you to hasten to the light and the rays
            of the Father,
            From whence was sent to you a soul endued with
            much mind.

            Z.   *Psel.* 33. — *Plet.* 6.

161.   Seek paradise.

            Z.   *Psel.* 20. — *Plet.* 12.

162.   Learn the Intelligible, for it subsists beyond the
            mind.

            Z.   *Psel.* 41. — *Plet.* 27.

163.   There is a certain Intelligible which it becomes
           you to understand with the flower of Mind.

           Z.   *Psel*. 31. — *Plet*. 28.

164.   But the paternal mind receives not her[16] will
           Until she has gone out of oblivion, and pronounce
           the word,
           Assuming the memory of the pure paternal
           symbol.

           Z.   *Psel*. 39. — *Plet*. 5.

165.   To these he gave the ability of receiving the
           knowledge of light;
           Those that were asleep he made fruitful from his
           own strength.

           Z. or T.   *Syn. de Insom.* 135.

166.[17]   It is not proper to understand that Intelligible
           with vehemence,
           But with the extended flame of an extended mind
           measuring all things
           Except that Intelligible. But it is requisite to
           understand this:
           For if you incline your mind you will understand

it
Not earnestly, but it becomes you to bring with
you a pure and inquiring eye,
To extend the void mind of your soul to the
Intelligible,
That you may learn the Intelligible,
Because it subsists beyond mind.

T.   *Dam.*

167.   You will not understand it, as when
        understanding some particular thing.

        T.   *Dam.*

168.   You, who understand, know the supermundane
        paternal depth.

        Z. or T.   *Dam.*

169.   Things divine are not attainable by mortals who
        understand body,
        But only as many as are lightly armed arrive at
        the summit.

        Z. or T.   *Proc. in Crat. — Tay.*

170.   Having put on the complete-armed vigour of
resounding light.
With triple strength fortifying the soul and the
mind,
He must put into the mind the symbol of variety,
and not walk
Dispersedly on the empyreal channels, but
collectively.

171.   For being furnished with every kind of armour,
and armed, he is similar to the goddess.

      T.   *Proc. in Pl. Th.* 324. — *Tay.*

172.   Explore the river of the soul, whence, or in what
order,
Having become a servant to body, you may again
rise
To the order from which you descended, joining
works to sacred reason.

      Z.   *Psel.* 5 — *Plet.* 1.

173.   Every way to the unfashioned soul extend the
reins of fire.

Z.   *Psel.* 11. — *Plet.* 24.

174.   Let the immortal depth of your soul lead you,
         But earnestly extend your eyes upwards.

         Z.   *Psel.* 11. — *Plet.* 20.

175.   Man, being an intelligible mortal, must bridle his
         soul,
         That she may not incur terrestrial infelicity but be
         saved.

                    Lyd. de Men. 2. — *Tay.*

176.   If you extend the fiery mind to the work of piety,
         You will preserve the fluxible body.

         Z.   *Psel.* 22. — *Plet.* 16.

177.   The telestic life, through a divine fire, removes all
         the stains, together with every foreign and
         irrational nature, which the spirit of the soul
         attracted from generation, as we are taught by the
         oracle to believe.

Z. or T.   *Procl. in Tim.* 331. — *Tay.*

178.   The oracles of the Gods declare, that, through
        purifying ceremonies, not the soul only, but
        bodies themselves become worthy of receiving
        much assistance and health: "for (say they) the
        mortal vestment of bitter matter will, by this
        means, be preserved." And this, the Gods, in an
        exhortatory manner, announce to the most holy of
        Theugists.

        Z. or T.   *Jul. Orat. V.* p. 334. — *Tay.*

179.   We should flee, according to the oracle,
        The multitude of men going in a herd.

        Z. or T.   *Proc. in I. Alc.* — *Tay.*

180.   Who knows himself knows all things in himself.

        Z.   1 *Pic.* p. 211. — *Tay.*

181.   The oracles often give victory to our own choice,
        and not to the order alone of the mundane
        periods. As, for instance, when they say, "On

beholding yourself, fear." And, again, "Believe yourself to be above body, and you are." And, still further, when they assert "That our voluntary sorrows germinate in us as the growth of the particular life we lead."

Z. or T.   *Proc. de Prov.* p. 483. — *Tay.*

182.   These things I revolve in the recluse temples of my mind.

183.   As the oracle, therefore, says, "God is never so much turned away from man, and never so much sends him new paths, as when he makes ascent to the most divine of speculations, or works, in a confused or disordered manner, and, as it adds, with unhallowed lips, or unwashed feet. For of those who are thus negligent, the progressions are imperfect, the impulses are vain, and the paths are dark."

Z. or T.   *Procl. in Parm.* — *Tay.*

184.   Not knowing that every god is good, you are fruitlessly vigilant.

Z. or T.   *Proc. in Pl. Pol.* 355. — *Tay.*

185.   Theurgists fall not so as to be ranked among the
        herd that are in subjection to fate.

                    Lyd. de Men. — Tay.

186.   "That the number nine is divine, receiving its
        completion from three triads, and preserving the
        summits of theology according to the Chaldaic
        philosophy, as Porphyry informs us."

                    Lyd. p. 121. — Tay.

187.   In the left sides of Hecate is a fountain of virtue,
        Which remains entire within, not sending forth its
        virginity.

            Z.   *Psel. 13. — Plet. 9.*

188.   And the earth bewails them even to their
        children.

            Z.   *Psel. 21. — Plet. 3.*

189.   The furies are the constrainers of men.

        Z.   *Psel.* 25. — *Plet.* 19.

190.   Lest being baptized in the furies of the earth, and in the neccesities of nature (as some one of the gods says) it should perish.

        Z. or T.   *Proc in Theol.* 297. — *Tay.*

191.   Nature persuades us that there are pure demons, Even the blossoms of evil matter are useful and good.

        Z.   *Psel.* 16. — *Plet.* 18.

192.   As yet three days ye shall sacrifice, and no longer.

        Z.   *Pic. Concl.* — *Tay.*

193.   In the first place, the priest, who governs the works of fire,
Must sprinkle with the cold water of the loud-sounding sea.

Z. or T.   *Proc. in Crat. — Tay.*

194.   Energize about the Hecatic Strophalus.

        Z.   *Psel. 9. — Nicep.*

195.   When you shall see a terrestrial demon
            approaching
            Exclaim, and sacrifice the stone Mnizurin.

        Z.   *Psel. 40.*

196.   If you often invoke me you shall see all things
            darkening,
            For neither does the convex bulk of heaven then
            appear,
            Nor do the stars shine, the light of the moon is
            hidden,
            The earth stands not still, but all things appear in
            thunders.

        Z.   *Psel. 10. — Plet. 22.*

197.   ....From the cavities
            Of the earth leap forth terrestrial dogs,

Shewing no true sign to mortal man.

Z. *Psel.* 23. — *Plet.* 17.

198. A similar fire flashingly extending itself into the
waves of the air,
Or even unfigured fire, whence an antecedent
voice,
Or light rich, glittering, resounding, revolved.
But when you see a horse glittering with light,
Or a boy, carried on the swift back of a horse,
Fiery, or clothed in gold, or naked,
Or shooting with a bow, or standing upon
horseback —

Z. or T. *Proc. in Pl. Polit.* 380.

199. When you behold a sacred fire without form
Shining flashingly through the depths of the
whole world
Hear the voice of fire.

Z. *Psel.* 14. — *Plet.* 25.

FRAGMENTS OF THE HERMETIC, ORPHIC, PYTHAGOREAN, AND OTHER COSMOGONIES AND THEOGONIES.

FROM THE ANCIENT HERMETIC BOOKS.

BEFORE all things that essentially exist, and before the total principles, there is one God, prior to the first God and King, remaining immoveable in the solitude of his unity; for neither is the Intelligible immixed with him, nor any other thing. He is established, the exemplar of the God who is the father of himself, self-begotten, the only father, and who is truly good. For he is something greater, and the first; the fountain of all things, and the root of all primary Intelligible existing forms. But out of this one, the self-ruling God made himself shine forth; wherefore he is the father of himself, and self-ruling: for he is the first principle and God of Gods. He is the monad from the one; before essence, yet the first principle of essence, for from him is entity and essence; on which account he is celebrated as the chief of the Intelligibles. These are the most ancient principles of all things, which Hermes places first in order, before the ethereal and empyrean gods and the celestial.

But, according to another division, he (Hermes) places the god Emeph[45] as the ruler of the celestial

---

[45] Generally supposed to be a mistake for Κνὲφ, Cneph.

gods: and says that he is Intellect understanding himself, and converting other intelligences to himself. And before this he places the indivisible One, which he calls the first effigies, and denominates him Eicton; in whom, indeed, is the first intellect and the first Intelligible: and this One is venerated in silence. Besides these, other rulers are imagined to exist, which govern the fabrication of things apparent: for the demiurgic Intellect, which properly presides over truth and wisdom, when it proceeds to generation and leads forth into light the inapparent power of the secret reasons, is called Amon, according to the Egyptian tongue: and when it perfects all things not deceptively, but artificially according to truth, Phtha; but the Greeks change the word Phtha into Hephæstus, looking only to the artificial: regarded as the producer of good things, it is called Osiris, and according to its other powers and attributes it has different appellations. There is also, according to them, another certain principle presiding over all the elements in a state of generation, and over the powers inherent in them, four of which are male, and four female; and this principle they attribute to the Sun. There is yet another principle of all nature regarded as the ruler over generation, and this they assign to the Moon. They divide the heavens also into two parts, or into four, or twelve, or thirty-six, or the doubles of these; they attribute to them leaders more or less in number; and over them they place one whom they consider superior to them all. Hence, from the highest to the last, the doctrine of the Egyptians concerning the principles, inculcates the origin of all things from One, with different gradations to the

Many; which (the Many) are again held to be under the supreme government of the One: and the nature of the Boundless is considered entirely subservient to the nature of the Bounded and the supreme Unity the cause of all things. And God produced Matter from the materiality of the separated essence, which being of a vivific nature, the Demiurgus took it, and fabricated from it the harmonious and imperturbable spheres: but the dregs of it he employed in the fabrication of generated and perishable bodies. — *Jambl.* sect. viii. c. 2. 3.

FROM THE MODERN HERMETIC BOOKS.

The glory of all things is God, and Deity, and divine Nature. The principle of all things existing is God, and the Intellect, and Nature, and Matter, and Energy, and Fate, and Conclusion, and Renovation. For there were boundless Darkness in the abyss, and water, and a subtile spirit, intellectual in power, existing in Chaos. But the holy Light broke forth, and the elements were produced from among the sand of a watery essence. — *Serm. Sac.* lib. iii.

FROM HORAPOLLO.

The world appears to them (the Egyptians) to consist of a masculine and feminine nature. And they engrave a scarabæus for Athena, and a vulture for Hephæstus. For these alone of all the Gods they consider as both male and female in their nature.

FROM CHÆREMON.

Chæremon and others believe that nothing existed prior to the sensible worlds, and they place among the foremost of such opinions the sentiments of the Egyptians, who hold that there are no other gods than those which are called the planets, and the constellations of the Zodiac, and such as these. They say, also, that the honours paid to the ten great gods and those which are called heroes, whose names appear in the almanacks, are nothing else than charms for the cure of evils, and observations of the risings and settings of the stars, and prognostications of future events. For it seems that they esteem the Sun to be the demiurgus, and hold that the legends about Osiris and Isis, and all other their mythological fables, have reference either to the stars, their appearances and occultations, and the periods of their risings, or to the increase and decrease of the moon, or to the cycles of the sun, or the diurnal and nocturnal hemispheres, or to the river: in short, that every thing of the kind relates merely to physical operations, and has no connexion or reference whatever to incorporeal and living essences properly so called. Most of them, also, suppose that some indissoluble connexion exists between our concerns and the motions of the stars, by a kind of necessity which they call Destiny, whereby all sublunary things are connected with these gods, and depend upon them. Hence they serve and honour them with temples and statues and the like, as the only beings capable of influencing Destiny. — *Eus. Pr. Evan.* iii. c. 4.

ORPHIC FRAGMENTS.

FROM ORPHEUS.[46]

Zeus is the first. Zeus the thunderer, is the last. Zeus is the head. Zeus is the middle, and by Zeus all things were fabricated.

Zeus is male, Immortal Zeus is female. Zeus is the foundation of the earth and of the starry heaven.

Zeus is the breath of all things. Zeus is the rushing of indefatigable fire.

Zeus is the root of the sea: He is the Sun and Moon. Zeus is the king; He is the author of universal life; One Power, one Dæmon, the mighty prince of all things:

One kingly frame, in which this universe revolves, Fire and water, earth and ether, night and day, And Metis (Counsel) the primeval father, and all-delightful Eros (Love).

All these things are United in the vast body of Zeus.

---

[46] Eusebius and Proclus omit the fifth and sixth verses between the parentheses. Aristotle places the fourth before the third.

Would you behold his head and his fair face,
It is the resplendent heaven, round which his golden locks

Of glittering stars are beautifully exalted in the air.
On each side are the two golden taurine horns,
The risings and settings, the tracks of the celestial gods;

His eyes the sun and the Opposing moon;
His unfallacious Mind the royal incorruptible Ether.

Eus. Pr. Ev. III. — Proc. Tim. — Aristot. de Mund.

FROM ORPHEUS.

First I sung the obscurity of ancient Chaos,
How the Elements were ordered, and the Heaven
reduced to bound;
And the generation of the wide-bosomed Earth, and
the depth of the Sea,
And Eros (Love) the most ancient, self-perfecting, and
of manifold design;
How he generated all things, and parted them from
one another.
And I have sung of Cronus so miserably undone, and
how the kingdom
Of the blessed Immortals descended to the thunder-
loving Zeus.

Arg. 419.

FROM ORPHEUS.

First (I have sung) the vast necessity of ancient Chaos,
And Cronus, who in the boundless tracts brought forth
The Ether, and the splendid and glorious Eros of a two-fold nature,
The illustrious father of night, existing from eternity.
Whom men call Phanes, for he first appeared.
I have sung the birth of powerful Brimo (Hecate), and the unhallowed deeds
Of the earth-born (giants), who showered down from heaven
Their blood, the lamentable seed of generation, from whene sprung
The race of mortals, who inhabit the boundless earth for ever.

Arg. v. 12.

FROM HESIOD.

Chaos was generated first, and then
The wide-bosomed Earth, the ever stable seat of all
The Immortals that inhabit the snowy peaks of Olympus,
And the dark aerial Tartarus in the depths of the permeable Earth,
And Eros, the fairest of the immortal Gods,
That relaxes the strength of all, both gods and men,
And subjugates the mind and the sage will in their breasts.
From Chaos were generated Erebus and black Night,

And from Night again were generated Ether and Day,
Whom she brought forth, having conceived from the
embrace of Erebus.
And Earth first produced the starry Heaven equal to
herself,
That it might inclose all things around herself.

Theog. v. 116.

FROM ARISTOPHANES.

First was Chaos and Night, and black Erebus and vast
Tartarus;
And there was neither Earth, nor Air, nor Heaven: but
in the boundless bosoms of Erebus.
Night, with her black wings, first produced an aerial
egg,
From which, at the completed time, sprang forth the
lovely Eros,
Glittering with golden wings upon his back, like the
swift whirlwinds.
But embracing the dark-winged Chaos in the vast
Tartarus.
He begot our race (the birds),[47] and first brought us to
light.
The race of the Immortals was not, till Eros mingled
all things together;
But when the elements were mixed one with another,
Heaven was produced, and Ocean,

-----

[47] This cosmogony is delivered by the Birds in the comedy so
called, and in this line they claim the priority of birth before the
gods as well as men.

And Earth, and the imperishable race of all the blessed Gods.

Aristop. Aves. 698. — *Suid. v. Chaos.*

FROM ORPHEUS.

Chaos and a vast yawning chasm on every side.

Tay.

"Maia, supreme of Gods, Immortal Night, tell me this,
How shall I constitute the magnanimous first
principles of the Immortals?"
"Surround all things with ineffable Ether, and place
them
In the mid Heaven."

Proc. Tim. 63.

ORPHIC HYMN TO PROTOGONUS.

I invoke Protogonus, of a double nature, great,
wandering through the ether,
Egg-born, rejoicing in thy golden wings,
Having the countenance of a bull, the procreator of
the blessed gods and mortal men,
The renowned Light, the far-celebrated Ericepæus,
Ineffable, occult, impetuous, all-glittering strength;
Who scatterest the twilight clouds of darkness from
the eyes,
And roamest throughout the world upon the flight of
thy wings,
Who bringest forth the pure and brilliant light,

wherefore I invoke thee as Phanes,
As Priapus the king, and as dazzling fountain of splendour.
Come, then, blessed being, full of wisdom and generation, come in joy
To thy sacred, ever-varying mystery. Be present with the Priests of thy Orgies.

FROM ORPHEUS.[48]

What Orpheus has asserted upon the subject is as follows: "From the beginning the Ether was manifested in time," evidently having been fabricated by God: "and on every side of the Ether was the Chaos; and gloomy Night enveloped and obscured all things which were under the Ether." by attributing to Night a priority, he intimates the explanation to be, that there existed an incomprehensible nature, and a being supreme above all others, and pre-existing, the demiurgus of all things, as well of the Ether itself (and of the night)[49] as of all the creation which existed and was concealed under the Ether. Moreover he says, "Earth was invisible on account of the darkness: but the Light broke through the Ether, and illuminated

---

[48] I have given this fragment from Malala, in whose text it appears to be less corrupted. It was originally preserved by Timotheus, who has evidently endeavoured to explain it upon Christian principles. His parenthetical explanations have been considered as part of the Orphic text, and been the cause of its obscurity. Without tampering with the text, I have endeavoured to restore it in the translation to its original purity. It is, doubtless, the same passage from the theogony of Orpheus, commented upon by Damascius. See infra.

[49] Omitted by Ced.

the Earth and all the material of the creation:" signifying by this Light, which burst forth through the Ether, the before-mentioned being who was supreme above all things: "and its name," which Orpheus learnt from the oracle, is Metis, Phanes, Ericepæus," which in the common Greek language may be translated will (or counsel), light, life-giver; signifying, when explained, that these three powers of the three names are the one power and strength of the only God, whom no one ever beheld, and of whose power no one can have an idea or comprehend the nature. "By this power all things were produced, as well incorporeal principles as the sun and moon, and their influences, and all the stars, and the earth and the sea, and all things that are visible and invisible in them. And man," says he, "was formed by this God out of the earth, and endued with a reasonable soul," in like manner as Moses has revealed. — *J. Malala*, p. 89. — *Ced. — Suidas v. Orpheus.*

FROM ORPHEUS.

Metis bearing the seed of the Gods, whom the blessed Inhabitants of Olympus call Phanes Protogonus.

In Crat.

And Metis, the first father, and all-delightful Eros.

In Tim. II. 102.

Soft Eros and inauspicious Metis.

Ib. 181.

Metis bearing the generation of the Gods, illustrious Ericepæus.

FROM ORPHEUS.

Orpheus has the following theological speculation in allusion to Phanes. Therefore the first God bears with himself the heads of animals, many and single, of a bull, of a serpent, and of a fierce lion, and they sprung from the primeval egg in which the animal is seminally contained.

Proc. in Tim.

FROM THE ANCIENT THEOLOGISTS.

The theologist places around him the heads of a ram, a bull, a lion, and a dragon, and assigns him first both the male and female sex.

Female and father is the mighty god Ericapæus.

To him also the wings are first given.

Proc. in Tim.

FROM THE ANCIENT THEOLOGISTS.[50]

They, the theologists, assert that Night and Heaven (Ouranus) reigned, and before these their most mighty father.

> Who distributed the world to Gods and Mortals,
> Over which he first reigned, the illustrious Ericepæus,

After whom reigned Night,

Having in her hands the excellent sceptre of Ericepæus,

After whom Heaven (Ouranus),

Who first reigned over the Gods after his mother Night.

FROM THE ANCIENT THEOLOGISTS.

In short, that to the power of the Sun is to be referred the control and supremacy of all things, is indicated by the theologists, who make it evident in the mysteries by the following short invocation.

Oh, all-ruling Sun, Spirit of the world, Power of the world, Light of the world. — *Macrob. Sat.* lib. i. c. 23.

---

[50] This extract from a MS. of Syrian is is given by Lobeck, Aglaophamus I. 577, and a translation of it with the Orphic lines from a MS. of Gale, was first given by Mr. Taylor, Class. Jour. XVII. 163.

PYTHAGOREAN FRAGMENTS.

FROM TIMÆUS LOCRUS.

Thus says Timæus the Locrian.—The causes of all things are two; Intellect, of those which are produced according to Reason; and Necessity, of those which necessarily exist according to the powers of bodies. Of these the first is of the nature of good, and is called God, the principle of such things as are most excellent. Those which are consequent, and concauses rather than causes, may be referred to Necessity, and they consist of Idea or Form, and Matter, to which may be added the Sensible (world), which is as it were the offspring of these two. The first of these is an essence ungenerated, immoveable, and stable, of the nature of Same, and the intelligible exemplar of things generated which are in a state of perpetual change: and this is called Idea or Form, and is to be comprehended only by Mind. But Matter is the receptacle of Form, the mother and female principle of the generation of the third essence, for, by receiving the likenesses upon itself, and being stamped with Form, it perfects all things, partaking of the nature of generation. And this Matter, he says, is eternal, moveable, and of its own proper nature, without form or figure, yet susceptible of receiving every form: it is divisible also about bodies, and is of the nature of Different. They also call Matter, Place and Situation. These two, therefore, are contrary principles; Idea or Form is of the nature of Male and Father; but Matter of the nature of Female and Mother; and things which are of the third nature are the offspring of the two. Since then there are three natures, they are comprehended in three different ways; Idea, which is the object of science, by Intellect; Matter, which is not properly an object of comprehension, but only of analogy, by a spurious kind of reasoning; but things compounded of the two are the objects of sensation, and opinion or appearance. Therefore, before the heaven was made, there existed in reality Idea, and Matter, and God the demiurgus of the better nature; and since the nature of Elder (Continuance) is more worthy than that of Younger (Novelty,) and Order than of Disorder; God in his goodness seeing that Matter was continually receiving Form and changing in an omnifarious and disordered manner, undertook to reduce it to order and put a stop to its indefinite changes, by circumscribing it with determinate figure: that there might be corresponding distinctions of bodies, and that it might not be subject to continual variations of its own accord. Therefore he fabricated this world out of all the matter, and constituted it the boundary of essential nature, comprising all things within itself, one, only-begotten, perfect, with a Soul and Intellect (for an animal so constituted is superior to one devoid of Soul and Intellect): he gave it also a spherical body, for such of all other forms is the most perfect. Since, therefore, it was God's pleasure to render this his production most perfect, he constituted it a God, generated indeed, but indestructible by any other cause than by the God who made it, in case it should be his pleasure to dissolve it.

FROM PLATO.

You say that, in my former discourse, I have not sufficiently explained to you the nature of the First. I purposely spoke enigmatically, that in case the tablet should have happened with any accident, either by land or sea, a person, without some previous knowledge of the subject, might not be able to understand its contents. This, then is the explanation, About the king of all things, all things are, and all things are on account of Him, and He is the cause of all good things. But the second is about things of the second kind, and the third about things of the third kind. Therefore the human soul, from its earnest desire to know what these things may be, examines those within itself which are akin to them, none of which it possesses in sufficient perfection. Such (imperfection) however is not the case with regard to the King and those natures of which I spoke, — *Plat. Ep. II.* p. 312.

FROM PLATO.

Conjuring the God of all things, the ruler of those which are, and are about to be, and the sovereign father of the ruler and cause. — *Plat. Ep. VI.* p. 323.

FROM AMELIUS.

Amelius makes the Demiurgus triple, and the three Intellects the three Kings — Him that *exists*, Him that *possesses*, Him that *beholds*. And these are different; therefore the First Intellect *exists* essentially as *that which exists*. But the Second *exists* as the Intelligible in him, but *possesses* that which is before him, and partakes altogether of that, wherefore it is the Second. But the Third *exists* as the Intelligible in the Second as did the Second in the First, for every Intellect is the same with its conjoined Intelligible, and it *possesses* that which is in the Second, and *beholds* or regards that which is the First: for by how much greater the remove, by so much the less intimate is that which *possesses*. These three Intellects, therefore, he supposes to be the Demiurgi, the same with the three kings of Plato, and with the three whom Orpheus celebrates under the names of Phanes, Ouranus, and Cronus, though, according to him, the Demiurgus is more particularly Phanes. — *Proc. in Tim. II.* 93.

FROM ONOMACRITUS.

Onomacritus, in the Orphics, says, that Fire, and Water, and Earth, were the first principles of all things. — *Sextus. Hyp. III.* 4. 136. — *Phys. IX.* 5. 6. 620.

FROM ION.

This, says Ion, is the beginning of my discourse. All things are three, and nothing more or less; and the virtue of each one of these three is a triad consisting of Intellect, Power, and Chance.

FROM PHILOPONUS.

Parmenides holds Fire and Earth primary principles: but Ion of Chios, the tragedian, placed them after Air. — *Philoponus.*

FROM PLUTARCHUS.

The moist nature, being the first principle and origin of all things from the beginning made the three first bodies, Earth, Air, and Fire. — *Plut. de. Is.*

FROM OCELLUS.

There are three boundaries, Generation, Summit, Termination. — I. 4.

FROM OCELLUS.

The first triad consists of Beginning, Middle, and End. — *Lyd. de Mens.* p. 20.

FROM PLATO.

Some say that all things consist of those which are in the course of generation, those generated, and those about to be generated; the first by nature, the second by art, and the third by chance. — *Plat. de Leg. X.*

FROM ARISTOTELES.

All things are three: for as the Pythagoreans say, the Universe and all things are bounded by three: for the

End, the Middle, and the Beginning, include the enumeration of every thing, and they fulfil the number of the triad. — *Aristot. de Cœlo. I.*

FROM ARISTOTELES.

The good and contemplative become so through three things; and these three are Nature, Habit, and Reason. — *Aristot. Polit. VII.*

FROM DAMASCIUS.

All things, therefore, are three, but not one; Hyparxis, Power, and Energy. — *Damas. Quæst.* c. 39.

COSMOGONY OF THE TYRRHENIANS.

A certain person among them, well versed in these matters, wrote a history, in which he says: That God, the demiurgus of all things, for the sake of giving dignity to his productions, was pleased to employ twelve thousand years in their creation; and extended these years over twelve divisions, called houses. In the first thousand years he created the heaven the earth; in the second he made all this apparent firmament above us, and called it heaven; in the third, the sea and all the waters in the earth; in the fourth, the great lights, the sun and the moon, together with the stars; in the fifth, every soul of birds, and reptiles, and quadrupeds, in the air, and in the earth, and in the waters: in the sixth, man. It appears, therefore, that the first six thousand years were consumed before the formation of man; and during the other six thousand years the human race will continue, so that the full time shall be completed even to twelve thousand years. — *Suid. v. Tyrrhenia.*

THE THEOGONIES.

FROM DAMASCIUS.

In the rhapsodies which pass under the name of Orphic, the theology, if any, is that concerning the Intelligible; and the philosophers thus interpret it. They place Chronus (Time) for the one principle of all things, and for the two Ether and Chaos: and they regard the egg as representing Being simply, and this they look upon as the first triad[51]. But to complete the second triad they imagine as the god a conceiving and conceive egg, or a white garment, or a cloud, because Phanes springs forth from these. But concerning this middle (subsistence) different philosophers have different opinions. Whatever it may be they look upon it as Mind; but for Father and Power some of them imagine other things which have no connexion with Orpheus. And in the third triad they substitute for it Metis, whilst they place Ericapæus as Power, and Phanes as Father.[52]

But the middle triad is never to be placed according to the triformed god (Phanes) as absolutely conceived

---

[51] The intelligible triad of the later Platonists was divided in three subsistences, each of which was also called a triad, and composed of subsistences bearing analogy to the whole.

[52] Wolf. and Lob. omit ὡς τὸν νοῦν. Taylor places it after Μῆτιν, and translates this very obscure passage thus: "But conceiving him over and above this as father and power, contributes nothing to Orpheus. But they call the third triad Metis as *intellect*, Ericapæus as *power*, and Phanes as *father*." I have inserted a full stop after προσήχοντα. Lob. does the same, though he gives no translation of the passage.

in the egg: for the middle subsistence always shadows out each of the extremes, as should this, which must partake at once both of the egg and of the triformed god. And you may perceive that the egg is the united (subsistence) or principle of union; and the triformed god, who is multiform about being, is the separated principle of the Intelligible; but the middle subsistence, being united as far as it relates to the egg, and already separated as far as it relates to the god, may be considered as existing altogether as in the act of separation: such is the common Orphic theology.

But the theology delivered by Hieronymus and Hellanicus is as follows: — He says that water was from the beginning, and Matter, from which the Earth was produced, so that he supposes that the two first principles were Water and Earth; the latter of which is of a nature liable to separation, but the former a substance serving to conglutinate and connect it: but he passes over as ineffable the one principle prior to these two, for its recondite nature is evinced, in that there is no manifestation appertaining to it. The third principle after these two, which is generated from them, that is from the Water and Earth, is a Dragon having the heads of a Bull and Lion naturally produced, and in the middle, between these, is the countenance of the God: he has, moreover, wings upon his shoulders, and is denominated incorruptible Chronus (Time) and Hercules. Fate also, which is the same as Nature, is connected with him, and Adrastia, which is incorporeally co-extensive with the universe, and connects its boundaries in harmony. I am of opinion that this third principle is regarded as subsisting according to essence, inasmuch as it is supposed to exist in the nature of male and female, as a type of the generating principle of all things.

And in the rhapsodies I conceive that the (Orphic) theology, passing over the two first principles, together with the one preceding those two which is delivered in silence, establishes the third, which is properly posterior to the other two, as the first principle, inasmuch as it is the first which has something effable in its nature, and commensurate with human conversation. For the venerable and incorruptible Chronus (Time) was held in the former hypothesis to be the father of Ether and Chaos: but in this he is passed over, and a Serpent substituted: and the threefold Ether is called intellectual, and Chaos boundless, and the dark cloudy Erebus is added to them as a third. He delivers, therefore, this second triad as analogous to the first, this being potential as was that paternal. Wherefore the third subsistence of this triad is dark Erebus, and its paternal principle and summit Ether, subsisting not simply but intellectually, and the middle derived from it is boundless Chaos. But with these it is said Chronus generated the egg, for this relation makes it a procession of Chronus, and born of these, inasmuch as from these procceds the third Intelligible triad. What, then, is this triad? The egg, the duad of the natures of male and female contained in it, and the multitude of the all-various seeds in the middle of it; and the third subsistence in addition to these is the incorporeal god, with golden wings upon his shoulders, who has the heads of bulls springing forth from his internal parts, and upon his head an enormous serpent, invested with the varied forms of beasts. This, therefore, is to be taken as the Mind of the triad: but the middle processions, which are both the Many and the Two, must be regarded as Power, but the egg as the paternal principle of this third triad. But the third god of this third triad, the theology now under discussion celebrates as Protogonus (First-born), and calls him Dis, as the disposer of all things, and the whole world: upon that account he is also denominated Pan. Such are the hypotheses which this genealogy lays down concerning the Intelligible principles.

But the cosmogony which is delivered by the Peripatetic Eudemus as being the theology of Orpheus, passes the whole Intelligible order in silence, as altogether ineffable and unknown, and incapable of discussion or explanation. He commences from Night, which Homer also constitutes his first principle, if we would render his genealogy consistent. Therefore we must not put confidence in the assertion of Eudemus, that Homer makes it commence from Oceanus and Tethys; for it is manifest that he regards Night as the greatest divinity, which is implied in the following line, where he says that she is reverenced by Jove himself —

He feared lest he should excite the displeasure of swift Night.

Homer, therefore, must be supposed to commence from Night.

But Hesiod, when he affirms that Chaos was the first produced, appears to me to regard Chaos as the incomprehensible and perfectly united nature of the Intelligible. From thence he deduces Earth[53] as the first principle of all the generation of the gods, unless, perhaps, he may regard Chaos as the second subsistence of the two principles: in which case Earth and Tartarus, and Eros (Love), compose the three-fold Intelligible, Eros being put for the third subsistence, considered according to its convertive nature. Orpheus also in his rhapsodies has adopted a very similar disposition, for he places the Earth for the first, being the first that was conglomerated into a compact and essential substance, while he places Tartarus as the middle, as having already, in a manner, a tendency towards disunion.

But Acusilaus appears to me to regard Chaos as the first principle and altogether unknown, and after this one to place the duad, Erebus as the male and Night as the female, the latter being substituted for infinity, and the former for bound; and from a connexion between these were generated Ether and Eros (Love), and Metis (Counsel), these three being the Intelligible hypostases, of which he places Ether as the summit, Eros as the middle in compliance with the natural intervention of love, and Metis as the third, inasmuch as it is already highly-venerable Intellect. And from

---

[53] The emendation of γῆν for τὴν is proposed by Mr. Taylor, and though I find no authority in the different texts for it, it is evidently requisite not only for the sense but to accord with Hesiod's Theogony.

these, according to the relation of Eudemus, he deduces the vast multitude of the other gods.

Epimenides affirms that the two first principles are Air and Night: whence it is evident that he reverences in silence the one principle which is prior to the two: from which, I conceive, he holds that Tartarus is generated regarding it as a nature in a manner compounded of the two; for some, indeed, regard the principle which is derived from these two as a kind of Intelligible intermediate subsistence or mediety, properly so called, inasmuch as it extends, itself to both extremities, the summit and the boundary; for by their connexion with one another, an egg is generated which is properly the very Intelligible animal from which again proceeds another progeny.

But Pherecydes Syrius considers the three first principles to be an Ever-vital subsistence, Chronus[54], and an Earthly subsistence; placing, as I conceive, the One prior to the Two, and the Two posterior to the One: and that Chronus generated from himself Fire, and Spirit, and Water, representing, I presume, the threefold nature of the Intelligible: from which, when they became distributed into five recesses, were constituted a numerous race of gods, called the five-times animated order, equivalent to what he might call a five-fold world. But another opportunity may perhaps occur for the discussion of this part of the subject. Such and of a similar description are the hypotheses which are received by us relative to the

---

[54] Χρόνον Mon. and Tay. which the following passage evidently requires.

Greek mythological fables, which are numerous and very various.

But the Babylonians, like the rest of the Barbarians, pass over in silence the One principle of the Universe, and they constitute Two, Tauthe and Apason; making Apason the husband of Tauthe, and denominating her the mother of the gods. And from these proceeds an only-begotten son, Moymis, which I conceive is no other than the Intelligible world proceeding from the two principles. From them, also, another progeny is derived, Dache and Dachus; and, again, a third, Kissare and Assorus, from which last three others proceed Anus, and Illinus, and Aus. And of Aus and Dauce is born a son called Belus, who, they say, is the fabricator of the world, the Demiurgus.

But of the Magi and all the Arion race, according to the relation of Eudemus, some denominate the Intelligible Universe and the United, Place, while others call it Time (Chronus): from whom separately proceed a Good Divinity and an Evil Dæmon; or, as some assert, prior to these, Light and Darkness. Both the one, therefore, and the other, after an undivided nature, hold the twofold co-ordination of the superior natures as separated and distinct, over one of which they place Oromasdes as the ruler, and over the other Arimanius.

The Sidonians, according to the same writer, before all things place Chronus, and Pothus, and Omichles, (Time, Love, and Cloudy Darkness). And by a connexion between Pothus and Omichles, as the Two principles are generated Aer and Aura (Air and a Gentle Breeze), substituting Air for the summit of the Intelligible, and the Breeze arising from it for the vivifying prototype of the Intelligible. And from these two again is generated Otus (the Night Raven), representing, as I conceive, the Intelligible Mind.

But independent of the collections of Eudemus we find the mythology of the Phœnicians thus delivered according to Mochus. First was Ether and Air, which are the Two first principles; from these was produced Ulomus, the Intelligible God, and, as I conceive, the summit of the Intelligible: from whom, by a connexion with himself, was produced Chousorus, the first expanding principle, and then the Egg: by the latter I imagine they mean the Intelligible Mind; but by Chousorus, the Intelligible Power, being the first nature which separates an unseparate subsistence, unless, perhaps, after the two principles the summit may be the one Wind; but to the middle, the two winds Lips and Notus (south-west and south), for sometimes they place these prior to Oulomus. In which case Oulomus himself would be the Intelligible Mind, and the expanding Chousorus the first order after the Intelligible, and the Egg Heaven: for it is said, that by the rupture of it into two parts heaven and earth were produced each from one of its two severed parts.

Of the Egyptian doctrines Eudemus gives us no accurate information. But the Egyptian philosophers, who are resident among us, have explained their occult truth, having obtained it from certain Egyptian discourses. According to them, then it appears to be this. The One principle of the Universe is celebrated as Unknown Darkness, and this three-times pronounced as such: and the Two principles are Water and Sand, according to Heraïscus; but according to Asclepiades, who is the more ancient of the two, Sand and Water, from whom, and next in succession after them, is generated the first Kamephis, and from this a second, and from this again a third, which, they affirm, completes the whole Intelligible distribution. Such is the system of Asclepiades. But the more modern Heraïscus says that the third, who is named Kamephis from his father and grandfather, is the Sun, equivalent in this case to the Intelligible Mind. But greater accuracy upon the subject can only be obtained from these authors themselves. It must be observed, however, with regard to the Egyptians, that they are often wont to distribute subsistences according to union, as when they divide the Intelligible into the individualities of a multitude of gods, as may be learnt from their own writings by those who will examine them: I refer particularly to the commentary of Heraïscus upon the Egyptian doctrine addressed to Proclus the philosopher alone, and to the concordance of the Egyptian writers, begun by Asclepiades and addressed to the other Theologists.

www.ingramcontent.com/pod-product-compliance
Lightning Source LLC
Chambersburg PA
CBHW051526050726
47503CB00014B/1998